D1254991

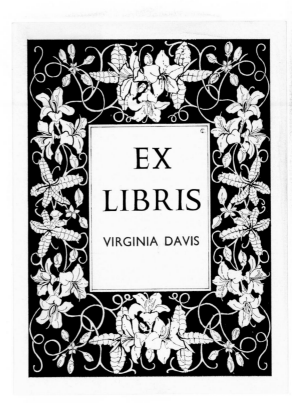

The Creative Art of Embroidery

Barbara Snook

HAMLYN
London · New York · Sydney · Toronto

Editor
Joan Fisher

The editor gratefully acknowledges the assistance of Christine
Hawkins with the preparation of this book, also the help and
co-operation so generously given by Mr. J. Clark, of J. & P.
Coats, Glasgow, and Mr. R. C. Yates, of Wm. Briggs, Bolton.

Published by
The Hamlyn Publishing Group Limited
London—New York—Sydney—Toronto
Hamlyn House, Feltham, Middlesex, England.

Printed by The Senefelder Printing Co. Ltd, Purmerend

Contents

Introduction

Embroidery is one of the oldest of crafts, and one of the most beautiful. Whether it is worked in a single colour with just one or two simple stitches on linen, or elaborate stitchery on velvet with gold thread and beads, each type of embroidery serves its purpose in adding richness and value to the article it adorns.

Basic materials for embroidery work are inexpensive. And the modest outlay on needles, threads and fabrics will quickly be redeemed in terms of hours of pleasure and creative satisfaction. Some of the most beautiful historic examples of embroidery, in fact, have been the work of peasants. Often crude materials were used because these were the only ones available, but the stitching was exquisitely worked, and the colours perfectly matched and contrasted. At the other end of the scale, magnificent works of art in stitchery have been created by noble and high-born needlewomen of the past.

By a careful choice of materials and threads, and of stitches themselves, embroidery can be used to reflect your way of life, your personality, your particular tastes in fashion, colour and design.

This book traces the fascinating development of embroidery since earliest times, and it serves as a guide to the principal categories of embroidery. The basic techniques are covered in full, with a dictionary of free embroidery stitches, and a guide to counted-thread work, cutwork, drawn-thread and drawn-fabric work. In the designs to make chapter you will find a varied selection of useful and decorative items to make.

Alas, lack of space prevents a detailed description of all the crafts allied to embroidery. The related subjects— appliqué, patchwork, collage, quilting, smocking and canvas work—have had to be omitted except where these subjects are relevant to the general history of embroidery. A smocked dress is however included in the designs to make (see page 164) with instructions for working the traditional smocking stitches used on the dress.

Some exciting experimental embroidery is being done today by experts and students, including new and individual interpretations of old ideas and techniques. The mixing of needlecraft techniques, and of hand and machine stitches, can add further dimensions to the craft. In modern embroidery, with all the resources of today's fibres and materials available to us, all things are possible.

Once you have acquired a working knowledge of stitches and techniques, and have begun to appreciate the value of colours and textures, you will inevitably want to go on to design for yourself. It is hoped this book will provide all the background information you need to take you through to this exciting stage.

How it all began

Embroidery is cloth decorated with needlework. Woven cloth was made even in prehistoric times and fragments of plaited and woven cloth from as long ago as 3000 BC have been found in several places in the world. Bone needles made by prehistoric craftmen have been found in the Brunique caves in France and bronze needles of about 2000 BC have been found in the Indus valley of India.

Flax was the first substance to be woven and linen was made by people in the early civilisations of Egypt, Syria, Palestine and Babylonia as well as many other places. The next fabric to be woven was cotton, which was first made into cloth in India and America, but was also known in the Near East in early times and in the later dynasties in Egypt. It was made in Greece in the time of Alexander the Great. Wool fabric has been found in Egyptian tombs and was also used by the Babylonians, but was more widely used in Asia. Silk was known to the Assyrians of the 7th and 6th centuries BC, and some may have come from silkworms. Tradition has it that silk was made into fabric in China as early as 2600 BC. By the time it reached the west, probably around the 3rd century BC, it was of a very fine quality.

It was because man needed to join pieces of cloth together that stitches developed. When these stitches were used for decorative and not purely utilitarian purposes embroidery had begun. Before man began to weave cloth he had used stitches to join the skins of various animals, first piercing holes with a needle then lacing the pieces together with overcast or whipped stitch and chain stitch—the same stitches which later were used decoratively in embroidery. North and South American Indians and Eskimos sewed porcupine quills and beads on to their skins to decorate them and African tribes decorated bark cloth—bark beaten until soft and like felt—and woven bark with stitches in early times. The early Egyptians of 6000 years ago were very skilled in basketwork. One form of basketwork was a type of weaving; the other was allied to needlework, again using overcast or whipped stitch. In basketwork can be traced evidence, too, of split stitch, then buttonhole, herringbone and many other embroidery stitches. All these activities were the forerunners of true embroidery.

Earliest examples

The earliest examples of embroidery have been found in Egyptian tombs, though for the most part the early Egyptians produced plain cloth, like that used for binding mummies. Paintings and carvings indicate that embroidery was worked; early tomb paintings show decorated couch covers, clothes, hangings and tents, and Egyptian sails were a form of patchwork. An ivory figure of a king, dated about 3400 BC, definitely

A Viking bone needle—relic of the early days of decorative stitchery.

suggests needlework on the king's mantle, most likely quilting. The tomb of Pharaoh Thothmes II, about 1500 BC, contained cloth with a papyrus and lotus blossom design, which may have been embroidered on or painted on.

Fabric found in the tomb of Thothmes IV was very fine woven linen with a tapestry-woven pattern of lotus in blue and red and papyrus in red, yellow and brown, both outlined with black. Warp threads were left bare especially so the design could be worked over them. A smaller piece of cloth from the same tomb was also tapestry, but a third piece, of coarser linen, was embroidered in satin stitch with linen thread, in a design of rosette-like forms, composed of six petals, some pink with green centres, some green with pink centres. This is one of the earliest pieces of true embroidery.

Most of the embroidery which has been found in Egyptian tombs dates from the Coptic period, beginning about the 1st century AD. These pieces show a Greek and Roman influence and by this time Christian symbols begin to appear in embroidery, particularly on tunics. Designs were executed in purples with details in stem stitch in natural-coloured linen thread. By the 4th and 5th centuries AD finer and more elaborate designs were worked with small touches of other colours, pinkish-red, yellow and green mainly. Embroideries were also worked in wool and the Coptic Egyptians made a lot of tapestry as well.

Early Egyptian pictures of foreigners show them dressed in ornate clothes and we know that the Babylonians were renowned embroiderers whose work was sought after throughout the east. A statue of Queen Napir Asu of 1500 BC indicates embroidery on her skirt and shawl. Babylonians and Assyrians attached great importance to wall hangings. Some of the larger hangings, depicting historical and mythological scenes, may have been composed of small pieces of appliqué embroidery. The Old Testament of the Bible mentions embroidery in several places and tells of gold plate and wire worked on fine linen in rich colours for liturgical garments. Gold thread was used about the 2nd century BC. Gold was beaten into thin sheets for spangles and for appliqué as well as into strips for thread.

The Greeks were skilled at weaving flax and though very few remains of embroideries from ancient Greece have been found, Homeric songs tell us how important an art it was and how much time was spent by Grecian women in embroidery. Statues from the Acropolis from the 6th century BC show decoration that looks like embroidery and scraps dating from the 4th century BC have been found from the Greek settlement at Kerch in the Crimea. These are of purple woollen cloth decorated with satin, knot and chain stitches. The Parthenon frieze shows the presentation of the peplos to Athens. Although the peplos— mantle—is not shown, perhaps because it would have been too difficult to recreate its splendour, we know that it was probably tapestry with a story-telling design. The presentation ceremony was performed every four years and once it was over the women immediately started work on making the next peplos.

Some of the Scythian embroideries found in Mongolia show similarities with the Greek embroideries from Kerch. The Scythians lived in south Russia about the 4th century BC and they traded with the Greeks. The walls of Scythian tombs were draped with embroidered hangings which showed a Greek influence. Excavations in the Altai mountains in Mongolia revealed woollen tunics, jackets and jerkins, the tunics covered with ornate appliqué designs. Women's clothes and belts, bags and satchels, and saddlecloths were also embroidered with appliqué, which became highly developed in the east.

Embroidery flourished in China long before any contact was made with the west, almost certainly as early as 1000 BC. Fragments of silk embroidery have been discovered in burial places along the ancient caravan route between China and the west which was used between the 7th century BC and the 2nd century AD. Woven silks, woollen tapestries and patchwork have also been discovered. Chinese embroideries of the T'ang dynasty (AD 618–906) have been found in Turkestan. An 8th century embroidered picture showing a life-size Buddha between two disciples and Bhosattras was discovered in a shrine at the Caves of the Thousand Buddhas. It is worked on a ground of fine buff silk, mounted on coarse linen, and embroidered with untwisted silks in satin and long-and-short stitches, with a little chain stitch and split stitch. Colours are light green, shades of red and blue, yellow, pink, grey, dark brown and indigo.

Some beautiful embroideries of over 2500 years ago have been discovered right on the other side of the world—in Peru. The Paracas embroideries, buried in graves beneath the sand of the coastal desert, were found in 1925. Among many other treasures, superb textiles were wrapped round mummy-bundles under layers of plain cotton cloth. Every weaving technique was represented and embroidered clothes, mantles, skirts, hats and bags were decorated with weird mythical creatures. Crayfish, butterflies, lizards, fish, flying birds, monkeys, cats and cat-faced men and warriors recur constantly. Bold colours were used: salmon pink, yellow, plum, blue, turquoise and navy on an ochre ground is just one of the many combinations. Wool from the llama, alpaca and vicuna and a little cotton thread were used, the most common stitch being stem, worked as a close filling or in rows. Chained border, satin, double running, encroaching stem and buttonhole also occur.

Development of silk weaving

By the 2nd century BC the caravan route from China to the west was carrying silk to the borders of Persia through Turkestan and Parthia. The Romans got silk from China and considered it very valuable. To make it go farther, it is thought, the Romans unravelled the silk, dyed it purple and then rewove it, though this effect could have been open needlework. The Romans so esteemed embroidery they called it 'painting with the needle'. Although there are no pieces in existence now, numerous paintings show decorated panels and appliqué work.

It was not until the 6th century that two monks smuggled silk

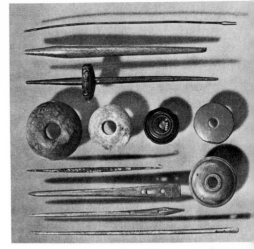
Selection of needles, looms and weights used in Roman times.

worms to Byzantium for Justinian I, which enabled the Byzantines to avoid the high Persian duties on Chinese silk. Then Byzantium became the centre for the production and distribution of cloth. Byzantine embroiderers, dyers and tailors were so tied to their work, they could not stop for even a minute unless someone took their place. From writings we know of highly decorated wall hangings, often with mythological beasts. Nothing in Europe matched the splendour of Byzantine embroidery until the 10th century AD.

The Arabs developed silk weaving in Sicily and Spain and so it spread throughout Europe, and Italy began to challenge Byzantium. In Ravenna is one of the earliest Italian embroideries, probably 8th century. This consists of short strips with embroidered portrait roundels on them, worked in silk against a couched gold background.

Another surviving early piece of European embroidery is English—the Durham stole and maniple. It was probably worked at the very beginning of the 10th century. It shows the prophets and saints and is worked in stem stitch, split stitch and couching, in red silk over very fine gold thread. Stitches completely cover the background. Embroidery was worked in England from Anglo-Saxon times and the embroidered curtains and hangings of the nobility were highly valued.

Early German embroidery was much influenced by Byzantine work. A group of magnificent early 11th century vestments may have been made in south Germany or possibly in Byzantium. On the cloak of St. Kenigund are great roundels filled with gold figures, and gold foliated patterns fill the spaces between. The

A 14th-century Chinese embroidered picture, representing one of the eight Taoist Immortals.

cloak of St. Stephen is comparable with the Bayeux tapestry which was made not many years later. Few remain of the secular wall hangings made to brighten interiors and reduce the chill of bare stone. A typical hanging tells the romance of Tristan and Iseult in simple appliqué work in woollen fabric with alternating red and blue squares.

Bayeux tapestry—a misnomer

The Bayeux tapestry is a true embroidery, not tapestry, being worked in wool on linen in laidwork and couching, with details in stem and outline stitches. The original is kept in France, but it was almost certainly worked in England. It tells the story of the Battle of Hastings and must have been started soon after 1066 when the incident was still fresh in the minds of the embroiderers. The linen is about 230 feet long and 20 inches wide and the colours used are shades of blue, indigo, red, green and yellow. These are used indiscriminately—a horse with matching hooves or legs is hard to find.

One of the finest embroideries in the world is the robe made at Palermo in Sicily in 1133. It was probably made for Roger II of Sicily, but later became the coronation mantle of the Holy Roman Empire. On the cope, back to back on either side of a date palm—a stylised Tree of Life—the lion of Christendom surmounts the vanquished camel of Islam. The robe is worked in gold thread, with some coloured silks, on a red silk ground. The whole outline was sewn with a double row of pearls, but extra jewels, enamels and motifs wrought in gold were added. Other Sicilian embroidery of the same period includes the 'Mantle of Charlemagne', with Byzantine displayed eagles in gold thread and silk on a red silk ground, heavily embroidered with pearls.

Opus anglicanum

During the 13th century English embroidery became outstanding and was known all over Europe. Ecclesiastical work between the mid-13th and mid-14th centuries was known as *Opus anglicanum* (English work) and is still known by this name. The work was so famous that copes, chasubles and other accoutrements of the clergy were commissioned as princely gifts and found their way into cathedral treasures all over Europe. The size of a cope is about 5 feet by 9 feet—a formidable area to cover with a design which had to appear the right way up from back and front when draped over the shoulders. Early copes were covered with scrolling stems and roundels, later with quatrefoils and arcading, and within these smaller divisions were biblical scenes worked in silk and gold. Each stitch was meticulously inserted into the background fabric, be it linen, silk or velvet.

Several characteristics distinguish *Opus anglicanum* from other contemporary work: fine gold backgrounds, diaper patterns in underside couching, dramatic gestures, skilled drawing of hands and feet, over-large eyes and elegant poses. Split stitch was used elsewhere in Europe and in China at this time, but not so finely worked. Few other stitches were used. The Butler-Bowden Cope, worked on velvet, and the Syon Cope, worked on linen, are famous relics of *Opus anglicanum*. The Syon Cope, probably made late in the 13th century, is completely covered with stitchery.

10

In medieval England other styles of embroidery flourished at the same time as *Opus anglicanum*, mainly developing from heraldry. While pennon, horses' trappings and surcoats on the battlefield were all embroidered, often heraldic artists' talents were put to use decorating sets of wall hangings and curtains with heraldic beasts, eagles, griffins and swans, and clothes with squirrels, rosemary, feathers and stars.

Elaborate embroidery with silk, gold and pearls similar to the ecclesiastical embroidery of medieval Europe was worked in Sweden. In the provinces rich materials masked weakness in drawing. Reliquaries covered in silk or linen, embroidered with gold couching, raised gold and silk, were vigorously designed but clumsily drawn. There are several 14th-and 15th-century church canopies of inlaid and applied work surviving. These are designed on a chequer plan in sombre shades of red, navy or green, brightened by white wool or linen. Animals occupy each chequer: lion, reindeer, unicorn, griffin and antlered lion.

Appliqué and inlaid work were also used for embroidered banners and palls in medieval times in Sweden and the same methods were in use also in Finland. Inlaid and applied woollen altar canopies were worked in mid and navy blue, with stitches mostly in white and pink. In Lapp territory in the extreme north, pliable birch bark was used as a background for applied fabric, the simple black patterns emphasised by the light, almost white, bark. In these northern countries with their long dark winters homes were gaily decorated with embroidered cushions, wall hangings and bed linen.

It is believed a school of embroidery flourished in Iceland, probably from the 12th century. An early piece of Icelandic embroidery in the Copenhagen National Museum depicts the Life of the Virgin. Embroidered in wool on coarse linen, the hands and faces are worked in chain and stem stitches, the background in laidwork and couching. The design is planned in roundels, a Byzantine method.

Above: the Butler-Bowden Cope, made around 1325, was worked on a velvet ground.

Opposite page: an example of Opus anglicanum—the back of a chasuble, showing the Tree of Jesse.

Drawing of an embroidered purse, from Town Ditch, Aldersgate, typical of designs worked in England in the 13th–14th centuries.

Appliqué work is found in early Italian embroidery too, but by the 12th century altar cloths were already being worked in white thread on white linen, using broad chain and stem stitches to outline diaper patterns set in a geometric layout. At least one 13th-century altar cloth shows the use of herringbone, satin and geometric satin stitches on counted threads. Whitework gradually came to include cut squares and needlepoint fillings.

One of the earliest records of needlepoint edging is shown in a Renaissance painting—a chemise with arabesque scrolling lines in gold on linen.

Changing styles in European work

On samplers experiments were made with small vandyke edgings in needlepoint and scattered motifs partly finished in blackwork, whitework and double running. Fragments of clothing show a love of detailed design and fine stitchery in both whitework and in coloured silks and metal thread. Sleeves and bodices were covered with small patterns. Methods used on domestic embroidery spread to other countries, mostly west and north of Italy.

A Byzantine style of figure drawing on early altar curtains eventually gave way to the stronger influence of contemporary painting, especially noticeable from the mid-14th century onwards in the pictorial embroidery of Florence. By the 15th century, natural-looking shading was being worked on these embroideries.

A typical Italian style was gold thread laid in rows and couched down with coloured silk, the spacing and colour of the silk stitches being arranged to shade the design. A piece in this style can be seen in the Museo dell'Opera del Duomo Florence: the small rectangular pictures designed for vestments by Antonio Pollaiulo which show the life of John the Baptist.

An Italian 16th-century linen band with cutwork and needlepoint lace fillings.

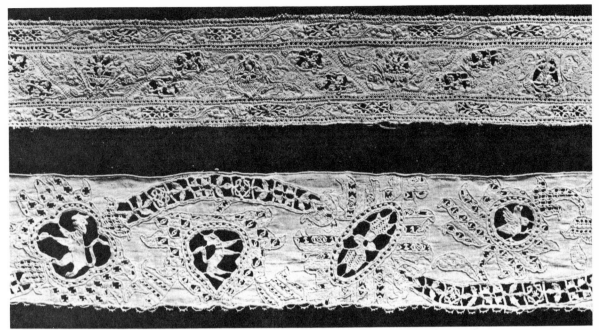

Another linen method used in Italy was Assisi work, often worked in red silk. Designs of acanthus foliage, beasts and occasional biblical and classical scenes were left void against a background of long-armed cross stitch, or a drawn-thread background of whipped stitch. Early pieces were seldom outlined with the double running we now associate with Assisi work.

Louis XI and Charles VIII of France were both very interested in embroidery and summoned Italian embroiderers to court, so early French work was much influenced by Italy. Ecclesiastical embroidery had been worked in the monasteries and convents but was never as fine as the contemporary *Opus anglicanum*. Early embroideries show that romantic narrative was as important as religious subject matter and records tell of the magnificence of French medieval costume, silk and velvet strewn with pearls and other jewels.

Bruges was to northern Europe what Florence or Venice was to the south. The luxury of the courts encouraged handicrafts and eventually embroidery came into common use in lay dress: the paintings of the Van Eyck brothers show embroidery on the costumes of this period. Some of the finest medieval ecclesiastical embroideries were worked in Flanders. Some fine whitework was made in Germany during the 15th century. Altar cloths in white linen were worked with white linen thread in several methods. Geometric satin stitch on a plain background, chain stitch on a drawn-thread background, stem, couching, plait, cross, open chain, herringbone, eyelet, darning, brick and a forerunner of Florentine stitch were all used on whitework.

During the 15th century there was a decline in English embroidery. After the magnificence of *Opus anglicanum*, the dissolution of the monasteries by Henry VIII and the subsequent redistribution of wealth and land led almost to a complete end to ecclesiastical embroidery. Embroideries from the church

Borders of whitework, cutwork and drawn-thread work made in Italy in the late 16th century.

Man's embroidered cap (top), and (below) a woman's embroidered bonnet, both examples of work done in the English Tudor era.

were cut up for household articles, the jewels were stolen and the gold melted down. There was a demand for embroidery in the home and household furniture, panels and cushions were embroidered. A knotted kind of stitchery on canvas, imitating Turkish carpets and known as Turkey work, came into use for chair and stool cushions.

Embroidery on costume

Costume styles in England and France had been similar for some time. A portrait of Henry VIII by Holbein shows him in a doublet with vertical bands embroidered with interlaced arabesques, probably outlined with couching. Arabesque designs came from Persia and Turkey by way of Venice, together with the magnificent velvets made in Venetian workshops. They appear in Clouet's painting of Francis I in which he wears a black velvet cloak embroidered with gold and silver arabesques.

When Francis I met Henry VIII at the Field of Cloth of Gold in 1520, much embroidery was worked for the occasion. Tents, banners, horse trappings, and men's costumes were decorated with splendid embroidery. Francis I wore gold and silver damask embroidered in coloured silk; his horse's mantle was of blue and gold tissue embroidery with *fleur-de-lis* in trellis work. Portraits of French women of the late 16th century show a high-necked gown with embroidery which looks like double running, a whitework collar, and a quilted bodice under a gown with revers finished with a small vandyke edging in needlepoint. Men's clothes were often black velvet with gold tracery touched here and there with colour. Domestic embroidery in France was mainly for the rich, with deep-piled velvets, rich brocades and heavy silks all embroidered with gold thread and coloured silks.

Spain, as well as Italy, formed an important channel through which Islamic design reached northern Europe. Sericulture (silkworm breeding) was introduced by the Moors, who dominated part of Spain from 711 to 1492, and flourished in the south. The workshops of Almeria had been, in the early 12th century, technically far ahead of those in northern Europe. Medieval Spain had also absorbed ideas from Eygpt, most notably double running embroidery. In Christian Spain ecclesiastical embroidery, influenced by the painting of France and Flanders, was rather stiff and burdened with gold—any bright silks were a Moorish influence.

By the 16th century Spaniards were setting the fashion, followed by Tudor men in England, of wearing trunk hose decorated with arabesque designs in gold and metal thread. In the north of Spain wool from abundant flocks of sheep provided the second important textile thread. Linen weaving had always been a Spanish handicraft and linens were much embroidered, particularly bedding, pillows and curtains for the marriage chest. Blackwork, black thread on white material, was in fairly general use on household linen. It often used undyed wool from the black sheep. Samplers, too, were an important record of blackwork. It is said Catherine of Aragon, Henry VIII's first wife, took blackwork to England where it became extremely popular in Elizabethan times.

A long pillow cover in Spanish blackwork, late 16th century.

Elizabethan period

The Elizabethan period is, in fact, the second great period of English embroidery. The arabesque was superseded by flowers and embroidery in coloured silks and metal threads; whitework blackwork, appliqué and canvas embroidery were all in use at the same time, and all were worked to a high standard. Patterns were in many cases professionally drawn, but the home embroiderer found inspiration from natural history books, flower paintings, and engravings. Many items of women's clothing were embroidered, in whitework, blackwork or coloured silks, sometimes with metal thread added. Men, too, dressed with ostentation. Their doublets and hose, gloves and shoes and cloaks were all embroidered. Shirts gradually became decorated with needlepoint edgings, drawn-thread work and heavier whitework.

In the home table carpets were worked in several ways: silk on canvas in tent stitch, silk and wool on canvas in long-armed cross stitch, Turkey work, and in couched metal thread on velvet. Designs were floral, heraldic or pictorial. Bed valances were generally worked in tent stitch, appearing from a distance like tapestry, the stitchery was so close. These bore mythological and biblical scenes.

The wall hangings at Hardwick Hall, in England, are now unique. The first set of five hangings, each 12 feet high, depict the Virtues, and are made in a patchwork of velvet and

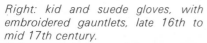

Right: kid and suede gloves, with embroidered gauntlets, late 16th to mid 17th century.
Below: man's linen nightgown, embroidered with silk and metal threads, early 17th century.

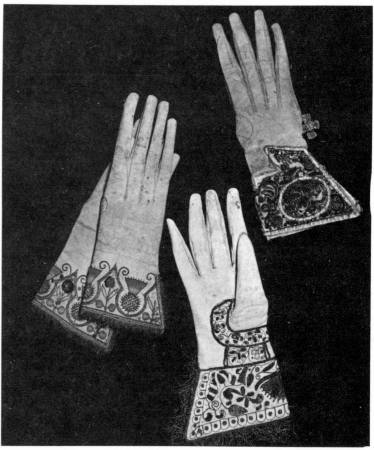

A child's traditional Portuguese Fiesta dress.

Right: examples of Yugoslavian traditional embroidery.
Below: a 19th-century Chinese embroidery, worked mainly in satin stitch.

cloth of gold and silver, outlined in cord, with details in appliqué and stitchery.

Chinese design began to affect Europe in the mid-16th century. In China silk tissues, brocades, velvets and tapestry-woven textiles were more important than embroidery, but embroidery was superb and executed perfectly. Floss and twisted silk, fine cord, silver and gold thread and gold twisted paper were the only threads used except in the poorest peasant work. The chief stitches were chain, satin, long-and-short, Pekinese, Chinese or Pekin knot (a tiny chained stitch), couching and laidwork, supported by split, straight, tent, brick, basket and some whipped stitches—a limited repertoire more than compensated for by the range of subtle colours. Every part of a design was symbolic. Imperial robes were embroidered with sacred symbols and only the emperor might wear all twelve. They included the sun with three-legged birds, stars and mountains. The robes took hours of constant work for four or five years.

When rich materials were embroidered with fine silks and gold and silver thread Chinese embroideries surpassed Byzantine and medieval ecclesiastical work. Embroidery on secular clothing also was symbolic: the peony was the symbol of spring, fish the symbol of fecundity, butterflies and bats symbols of happiness.

A Jacobean long cover in linen, embroidered with coloured silk in long and short, stem, herringbone and satin stitches, with laid and couched work. Rows of sprig motifs form an important part of the design.

The Indian influence

India also influenced European work and embroidery was worked there from early times. The earliest surviving pieces are late 16th century and are Mogul, a blend of Indian and Persian embroidery, which arose from the demands of court fashion. The Mogul emperors encouraged Persian embroiderers to settle in India. Court costume, sprigged turban cloths and girdles, floral prayer mats, pictorial hangings and tent panels were all worked in coloured silk, sometimes in great detail. Embroidered coverlets, which later affected European design, found their way to Europe long before the trade reached its peak in the late 17th and early 18th century. The flowering tree motif, originally Chinese, appealed to western eyes and Indian embroiderers adapted their designs, even working to European specifications, though these were modified by strong native tradition.

Persia, geographically midway between east and west, provided a channel through which ideas flowed between Europe, India and China. Woven textiles, brocades and carpets were of more importance than needlework in Persia, but Persian design spread to other countries—arabesques from metal dishes and spouted water jars found their way to Europe in the 16th century, flower sprigs from quilted mats in the 18th century and the cypress tree travelled east to Kashmir and west through Turkey to Epirot Greece. Covers, prayer mats and bath rugs in coloured silks on a white ground, sprinkled with flowers and surrounded by several chain-stitch borders, and quilted in trellis or overlapping circles, influenced Indian printed textiles which in turn affected the design of 18th-century English coverlets.

Marco Polo wrote about Persian embroidery in the 13th century, but none earlier than the 16th century exists today. Prayer and bath mats, carpets, robes, hangings, curtains and table covers were all embroidered. Early embroideries covered the entire ground, floral patterns were very popular and birds the only living being frequently represented. Styles varied in different parts of the country but included double darnings, cross stitch and applied and inlaid work, the last having a mosaic effect.

As in Persia and other eastern countries, Turkish textiles were more highly thought of than needlework. The earliest reference is to silk headshawls in the 16th century. Much clothing was elaborately embroidered—red and purple dresses decorated with gold were very popular and men's long kaftans, trousers and coats were all decorated. Among many household items—cushions, napkins, bedspreads, bath mats, prayer mats and so on—which were embroidered were loosely woven linen towels.

The embroidery looks heavy because of the coarse twisted silk and metal thread, though some of the floral patterns look fragile. The two main styles of Turkish embroidery—floral patterns on cotton or fine linen and heavy gold on velvet—lasted over the centuries. Decoration reached a climax in the 17th and 18th centuries, however, when even horses' harnesses had gold and silver embroidery.

The Portuguese brought home embroidery from the east

An example of drawn-thread work from 17th-century Italy—a linen sampler which is signed Gullia Piccolomini.

earlier than other Europeans; from the 15th century onwards they had imported eastern goods, particularly bedspreads. Persian carpet designs were copied, too, but eventually eastern ideas blended with the traditional designs. In the early 17th century Renaissance styles predominated, with embroidery in silk on velvet, using French knots, satin and brick stitches, couching and laidwork and applied cord. Similar stitches were used with velvet appliqué on satin in dark colours, with couched silk cord added. Whitework in silk on linen designed in a lighter vein was often pictorial, with animals, trees and people, similar to contemporary English work. A wide selection of stitches included coral, satin, back, oriental knotted feather, French and bullion knots, whipped herringbone, Portuguese knotted stem, and cable. Rural areas had the gayest and most original embroidery—Alentejo was celebrated for its bridal bedspreads and Arraiolos for its needlework carpets worked in long-armed cross.

Needlework pictures

In Europe in the 17th century, furniture came to be embroidered more and more. English needlework pictures were worked in silk and metal thread on linen which allowed tent stitch to be worked next to surface stitches. Biblical, classical and allegorical stories were worked with characters dressed in

Right: a stumpwork tray, 17th century. Below: a Jacobean bed, 1615—20, with hangings embroidered with crewelwork.

contemporary court costume. Embroideries wholly or partly in stump work, bead work, tent stitch with biblical scenes, or impractical satin stitch in silk on a white silk ground were made into table cabinets.

Three new styles emerged. Firstly samplers, which began in the late 16th century, took hold in the 17th. The earliest were short and broad, worked in coloured silks and metal thread on loosely woven linen. Scattered motifs of birds, animals, trees, flowers and geometric patterns were used, with back, plaited braid, tent, cross, Algerian eye and other canvas stitches. Other samplers were long and narrow, occasionally signed and dated, worked in silk on soft linen, sometimes with whitework, cut-work and openwork. Another type was entirely whitework with geometric satin stitch, drawn-thread work, needleweaving and needlepoint fillings.

Stumpwork did not acquire this name until the 19th century. The Elizabethans had worked a version of raised work, but in the 17th century wooden moulds were covered with button-hole stitch, then horsehair and wax were added. Subjects were classical and biblical with characters in contemporary dress again. Objects, people and animals, regardless of scale, scattered across padded hills and coloured purl grass. Pictures, mirror frames and caskets were all treated in this way.

Crewel embroidery, too, acquired its name later; in the 17th century it was called Jacobean wool work. It was used for bed curtains and other large hangings, usually worked on a stout fabric with a linen warp and cotton weft. There were two main styles: one, reminiscent of Elizabethan design, had scrolling patterns of leaves and flowers and coiling growths, the other, larger, group was oriental-inspired, with shaded colours.

Early American embroidery

Crewel wools were taken to America by the early settlers, along with embroidery techniques from many countries—all European methods were introduced, but limited resources enforced

A quilted christening robe, mid 18th century.

Top: patchwork coverlet made in the second half of the 19th century in America. Printed cotton has been used to form a Star of Bethlehem pattern. Above: Chinese embroidered collar, late 19th century.

adaptations. Long before the arrival of the settlers and explorers the Indians in America had decorated skins—otter, beaver, sheep, doe, buck, elk and bison—with porcupine quills and beads. Shades of red, blue, green, purple, brown and white dye were obtained from native plants. The quills were couched with fine thread sinew first in traditional geometric and stylised patterns, later in floral and other designs.

Beads, made originally of crude minerals, seeds, horn, bone and shell, were strung in short lengths and attached to skin or trade cloth by couching in solid areas of colour.

Crewel embroidery worked by the settlers was far lighter than in England and less influenced by Indian and Chinese fabrics. Floral designs were embroidered on clothes and on household articles. Experiment with berries, vegetables, bark and plants produced a good range of dye colours—blue was the most common. Only about a dozen stitches were in common use: bullion and French knots, chain, couching, couched fillings, cross stitch, fly, herringbone, Roumanian, satin and surface satin, seeding and stem.

The freer floral style spread through all types of embroidery, in the 18th century, including canvas work. But apart from crewel work the other embroidery technique which became outstanding in America was quilting. The all-white quilt, using essentially the same technique as in Europe, reached its peak in the late 18th century. Finely stitched, intricate patterns had a wide assortment of names and sometimes historical significance.

Patchwork originated from necessity: only families with reasonable access to the eastern seaboard could obtain fabric easily. To those who had pioneered inland every scrap of material was precious. From humble beginnings grew a great array of designs—over 200 names have been recorded. As more material became available the applied quilt gained in popularity over the pieced quilt. The simplest patterns were based on a folded square, divided into triangles and rectangles (goosetracks). At the end of the 18th century embroidery in white French knots and fine cord became transformed by American women into candlewicking for use on summer cotton quilts. Loops of wicking were made by taking running stitches over twigs or turkey bones. In early work these loops were sometimes left uncut.

18th-century techniques

Chinese influence on embroidery design in Europe reached its climax in the 18th century. By this time Chinese embroiderers worked for the European market, exporting to England, France, Portugal and Spain. Sometimes designs were commissioned which included heraldic blazons alien to oriental culture, but these often retained marked Chinese characteristics. Europeans seized upon Chinese motifs—peony, pomegranate, butterflies, deer, phoenix and dragon—heedless of their symbolic meaning in China.

In England, where interest in floral design was already firmly established, reaction against heavy crewel work brought much lighter and more delicate designs in silk. Simultaneously the influence of Dutch flower painting and French vases of more stylised plants can be seen in much English work. Quilting was worked there, too, both for clothes and furnishings.

In the 18th century French work was superior of that of other European countries and so much in demand in them. Men's coats were exquisitely worked in floral designs inspired by India, China and Persia. All embroidery was in silk, in long-and-short, satin, chain and tambour work together with tinsel, sequins and pearls. Bed hangings and upholstery were also floral with much Chinese influence, and delicately worked in tent or cross stitch on canvas or in silk on satin. Mythological scenes were also worked. In the French revolution many embroideries were destroyed or had their gold and silver thread picked out. Afterwards little embroidery was worked—none on men's clothes and only on sheer fabrics for women's clothes which were embroidered with scattered flowers.

Forerunners of Berlin woolwork designs, which made a great impact in the 19th century, appeared in Portugal at the end of the 18th century. One design showed a bouquet of flowers and a wreath; another a plate of food complete with knife and fork, glass and bottle of wine.

Whitework from Saxony in Germany was taken to Edinburgh in 1782 by an Italian embroiderer where it gave rise to Ayrshire work—fine muslins, cambrics and linen were embroidered in white cotton for collars and cuffs and so on. There was a great demand for lacy embroidery and Ayrshire work became very popular. It was still used for baby's clothes, christening robes and

Above: silk dress with Chinese embroidery, 1775–80.
Below: an example of whitework, from 18th-century France—the white silk cover is embroidered with white silk threads.

Above, left: green taffeta apron, embroidered with gold and silver, 1718. Above, right: a 19th-century pincushion with traditional floral design.

veils in the mid-19th century in England, but *broderie anglaise* was the fashionable trimming for many women's clothes, particularly underwear. *Broderie anglaise* was less delicate than Ayrshire work which, embroidered on muslin, appeared very fragile.

The standard of whitework in France in the 19th century was extremely high as well. Drawn-thread work on fine cambric had many different filling stitches and almost invisible speckling, worked in fine cotton. *Kasida* embroidered muslins from India became the vogue in France, England and America in the 19th century. Muslins were woven at Dacca; those embroidered with white cotton in darning and satin stitch were called *chikan*, and those embroidered in gold and coloured silks, also in darning and satin stitch, were called *kasida*. Other work in India at this time included Cutch embroidery for skirts and festive cloths which made use of dark grounds and thread—navy. deep red or turquoise green—with white thread showing up brilliantly in contrast. Interlacing stitch and chain stitch were much used.

The Berlin woolwork era

The most important needlework fashion in the 19th century was Berlin woolwork, which swept through England and America and was tremendously popular for thirty years. Bright colours and sentimental subjects—pet dogs, pictures of royal pets, and bouquets of roses are just some—were the outstanding features. Designs were copied from coloured patterns first published in Berlin in about 1805 and imported in large quantities by a London shop in 1831. At first pictures were worked entirely in cross and tent stitch with worsted wools, but soon details were added in clipped wool, cut-steel beads, jewels, pearls and sequins. Eventually every conceivable small article, upholstery, rugs and carpets were all embroidered. At last geometric patterns and softer colours began to appear again in the 1860s.

American women worked Berlin woolwork too, though they added coloured glass beads and finished off with heavy silk cords, tassels, ribbons, bows and fringes. It was also worked on perforated cardboard for bookmarks, greeting cards and wall

Below: an example of darning on net.

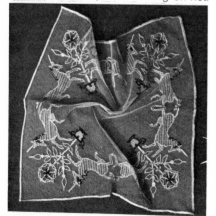

Cotton petticoat, trimmed with broderie anglaise, 1850—70.

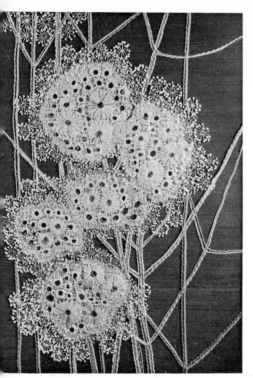

'Cow Parsley', a modern embroidered panel of delicate stitchery, with beading and drawn-thread work, and a variety of stitches including couching, laid threads, chain and French knots.

mottoes. Other methods in use in America in the 19th century were darning on net and embroidery on muslin (for which patterns were given in women's magazines), Mountmellick work (an Irish version of Ayrshire work) and *broderie anglaise*. In the late 19th century there was a revival of crewel work, which had died out when cheap printed fabrics were available, and crewel designs were sometimes now worked in silk on woollen fabric or velvet.

Buttons probably reached America in the mid-19th century and were used by the Indians on the north-west coast for their button blankets. These kept to traditional designs: red flannel was applied to heavy black blanket cloth with hemming and the motif drawn with pearl buttons and white beads. On Chilcat blankets, the ceremonial robes of the Tlingit Indians, a border of two or three rows of stem stitch in varied shades outlined the woven pattern and could justifiably be called embroidery. The blankets were woven with a goat wool weft on a shredded cedar bark warp. The stem stitch outline neatened the pattern in beautiful shades of turquoise, yellow and natural white and black.

Present-day embroidery—a fresh approach

While traditional embroidery, particularly tent stitch, crewel work and quilting, continue to be popular in America, an increasing amount of purely experimental work has been, and is being, done. One development of the 20th century has been shaded silk embroideries. Worked on white linen with fine silks, designs of floral sprays, garlands, birds and butterflies are delicately shaded.

With the development of machinery and different kinds of material, embroidery declined from the mid-19th century onwards. Scandinavia has contributed most to the promotion of good design in the 20th century. A revival of interest in embroidery started in Denmark in the 1920s. While most of modern Danish influence has been in the field of drawn-fabric work, cross-stitch designs have also received new treatment. Danish cross-stitch designs of wild flowers in natural colours, often using eight or more shades in a single design, whether used on table mats, cushion or aprons and worked in stranded cottons on linen or wool on coarser material, have shown that cross stitch need not be restricted to use on canvas or to purely geometric or conventional patterns on linen.

In modern Finland much work has been done with drawn fillings for stitches on loosely woven linen. Some Finnish sheer woollen gauzes make excellent surfaces for drawn-fabric work in linen floss, embroidery cotton and crewel wool. The impact of modern Scandinavian design on England and America has been very marked. Designs, often based on simple motifs—some of them derived from peasant work—continue to be worked with a limited number of stitches and an outstanding range of colours, though each work is usually carried out in a restricted colour scheme.

The revival in embroidery design in England gained impetus after the second world war. Opportunities for ecclesiastical work were provided by the building of new churches and man-made material and fibres and untarnishable threads have enabled

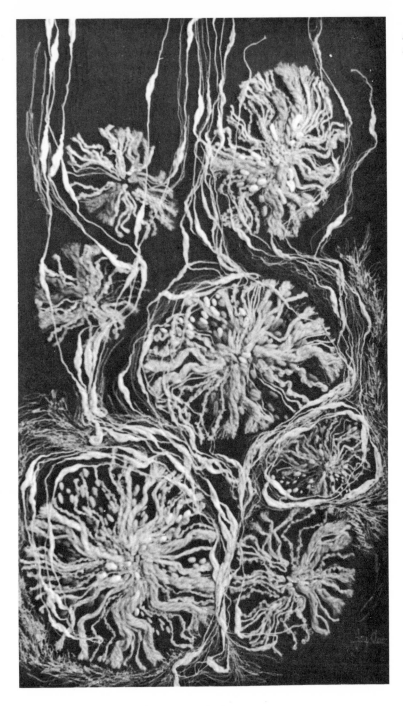

more experimentation to be carried out.

Embroidery is no longer a matter of known stitches on familiar fabric. Designers are striving for new textural effects, new colour and thread relations and stitchery, in some work, is lost. While some designers specialise in ecclesiastical embroidery, bead and gold work, embroidered collage or needlewoven tapestries, with fabrics applied above and below the original surface and all manner of substances attached, others use no one technique alone, and experimentation seems endless.

National embroidery styles

NORWAY

Norwegian embroidery generally brings to mind Hardanger work, but this is only one branch of the craft. In a country so divided by fjord and mountain, with strong regional characteristics, it is surprising that a national style should have evolved. In the 18th century a renewal of peasant arts was stimulated by Renaissance ideas, though the inaccessible areas such as Telemark and Setesdal were less affected than Oslo and Gudbrandsdal. The acanthus, which from 1700 dominated wood carving around Oslo, spread to country districts and to embroidery design. The Hallingdal and Telemark districts favoured rose painting on wood, which in turn spread to embroidery. On the west coast whitework and other counted-thread methods remained more popular. Rose embroidery, 'rosesom', is fairly widespread, possibly taken from one place to another by itinerant professional embroiderers. Swirling patterns, sometimes of leaves and flowers, are worked in shaded rows of satin stitch, at times separated by stem or back stitch.

In Norway women's peasant costume comprises blouse, sleeveless bodice, apron and a variety of headdresses. About one hundred and fifty different costumes can still be seen on festive occasions.

A linen towel from Telemark, Norway, with embroidery worked in wool in cross, satin, stem and Holbein stitches, patterned darning and plaited fringe, 18th century.

English 19th-century croquet dress.

Hardanger work sampler.

Gudbrandsdal costume was influenced by town styles earlier than other neighbourhoods. Rococo flowers in bright colours scattered over the skirt are surrounded by a wide border. Blue cap, bolero and purse are embroidered to match the skirt and the blouse is decorated with whitework.

Telemark costumes are a little more restrained, but still very richly decorated in 'rosesom' and vine tendrils. Strong colours are used: red and green on black, dark blue or green woollen cloth for jacket, skirt and bolero, though the last can sometimes be in red. The white blouse has 'rosesom' too at wrists, on neckband and down the front.

Heddal costume is in bright red and blue cloth. The red jacket has a narrow band along the edge and down the opening, which is also repeated at the wrists. The blue cloth apron has a floral border which runs along the hem and about one foot up each side. The white blouse repeats the coloured floral embroidery on wrists and neckband and down the front. The **Hallingdal** district uses 'rosesom' more densely on shoulder straps, waistband, narrow hem, border and cap in bright wools on dark cloth.

At **Voss**, applied felt makes the border pattern on the skirt. The large white headdress is embroidered with scattered motifs in cross stitch, patterned darning and Holbein stitch in black silk. Blouse collar, front and wrist bands have a black and white star pattern, the apron border is white counted satin and black cross stitch while the stomacher is red, black and white.

Hardanger costume is distinguished by the elaborate stomacher worked in cross-stitch geometric patterns, a similarly bold waist belt which sometimes has beads added and the well-known whitework which adorns the full-length apron in a wide border.

Hardanger work

Hardanger embroidery is an elaborate form of whitework on linen. It is suggested that Italian and German 16th and 17th-century pattern books influenced designs, yet if so the embroidery which evolved soon developed its own motifs and a regional style emerged.

Hardanger work decorates collars, cuffs, neckbands and front openings of blouses, headdresses and wide borders on long aprons worn for gala occasions. The style has spread beyond Norway but elsewhere it is mainly used for decorating table linen. Traditional border patterns include the following white-work methods: cutwork, drawn-thread hem stitch, and geometric satin stitch. Chained border, four-sided and eye stitches are also used. Cut and drawn patterns are worked on a 'cut four, leave four' basis, cut threads being protected by blocks of five satin stitches, worked before threads are cut and removed. The remaining threads are turned into bars, neatened by whipping and weaving.

DENMARK

There are two styles of Danish whitework. One follows very closely the design and method used at the end of the 19th century: conventionalised flowers have for their curved outlines two rows of chain stitch worked in coarse thread. These make a strong contrast to the drawn-thread work fillings. Whitework such as this is used on hand-woven table linen, guest towels, tea cosies, chair backs and cushion covers. It can sometimes be worked in one shade of pink or blue with whitework. The second style is worked on loosely woven linen 'scrim'. Curved shapes outlined with chain stitch are still used, but generally design relies on rectangular shapes with drawn-fabric fillings.

Hedebo work

Hedebo is the traditional Danish embroidery on white linen and is seldom worked in any other country. In Denmark it belongs particularly to a locality south-west of Copenhagen. It probably began during the Renaissance but the earliest remaining pieces date from the mid-18th century when, as a peasant craft, Hedebo was used to decorate the trousseau.

A girl worked a shirt for her future husband and a chemise, aprons and underclothes for herself, plus pillow-cases, towels, bedcovers and other household linen.

The oldest work is arranged in bands of drawn-thread fillings with motifs taken from Renaissance furniture and scrollwork from books. By the 19th century geometric designs had become less rigid and stylised: plants, leaves, flowers and stars and figures from Paisley shawls were introduced. Designs, drawn on the linen, were heavily outlined with chain stitch before fillings were worked in linen thread. When cotton was introduced designs grew correspondingly lighter and stem and satin

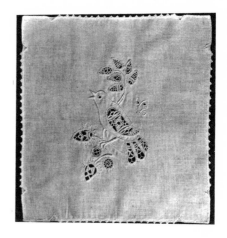

Above: Hedebo sampler.

Below: examples of Swedish work. On right of picture, linen cap bands from Scania district, showing needle-weaving with bobbin lace, early 20th century. On left of picture, a cotton neckerchief from Dalecarlia district, with embroidery worked in silk in satin and cross stitches, 1840.

stitches were added to the stitch repertoire. A further change took place in the mid-19th century when holes were cut in the fabric and filled with buttonhole stitchery, made into bars, picots and circular motifs.

SWEDEN

Different districts, Dalecarlia in central Sweden, Blekinge in the east and Scania in the south, developed their own local styles for embroidery in the home.

The use of cross stitch, sometimes with long-armed cross, on linen is widespread. Coloured threads, used for men's wedding shirts and neckcloths as well as cushions and bed linen, often are two or three shades of pink and blue used together. Holbein stitch was also used for clothes. Combined with geometric satin and cross stitches, it seems often to have been worked in black silk on white linen. Geometric satin, though, is generally associated with whitework. It appears on shirt neckbands, collars and cuffs, particularly in Dalecarlia, both on its own and with drawn-thread work.

In drawn-thread and drawn-fabric work, beautiful designs composed of a few simple motifs are embroidered in hem stitch, four-sided stitch, needleweaving and filling stitches. These contrast with star patterns worked in geometric satin stitch.

Free embroidery in wool occurs throughout the country on chair and long carriage cushions, worked in stem, French knots, various fillings and long-and-short stitch. Gaily coloured flowers and leaves with occasional animals are placed on a dark ground. The carriage cushions of Scania are renowned; the best of these were made before the mid-19th century. Similar designs are found on red coverlets, where, although some shading is attempted, variation in dye and the roughish texture of wool and stitchery evidently seemed enough to most needlewomen.

PORTUGAL

While some methods are known throughout the country certain districts have developed distinct regional styles.

In **Castelo Branco** work, eastern influence appears in scrolling designs which spring from a central stem, similar to the Tree of Life motif. The two-headed eagle and other birds are used—a bird may have a floral wing and a leafy tail.

Bridal bedspreads, usually with a border and central medallion, valances and curtains are worked in home-spun, home-dyed floss silk. Surface satin stitch, couched at regular intervals, is known as Castelo Branco stitch in Portugal.

Embroidery from **Viana do Castello** is very lively. Designs are based on recurring motifs, which, if not drawn from memory, are traced round simple templates: hearts, clover leaves, lover's knots, urns, leaves, flowers and buds. Red flannel skirts, pockets and bodices are embroidered in white knitting cotton. Other garments, in blue woollen cloth, are worked in coloured wool and cotton with large loose stitches, while gala clothes have sequins, beads and gold lace added. Similar designs appear on table linen and cushion covers in blue thread on white ground, red on white, or both red and blue on white. In this work drawn-thread fillings are used in leaf and heart shapes. Stitches include

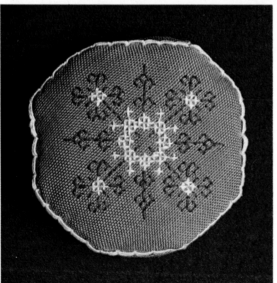

Above: Greek table mat worked in cross stitch.
Left: pincushion showing a combination of cross stitch and Assisi work.

Opposite page: 'The Three Kings', an embroidered picture incorporating various counted threads and other stitchery, also laid gold threads.
Left: Portuguese table mat.

straight, satin, crown, encroaching satin and closed herringbone.

Guimarães, in the **Minho**, specialised in whitework peasant shirts, a combination of narrow drawn-thread bands, eyelet holes and bullion knots in simple geometric patterns.

Shaped bands of thick, coarse, natural linen applied by hemming to peasant waistcoats are worked in red and blue buttonhole, detached chain, seeding, dot and satin stitch. Other embroideries of the Minho province include unbleached linen bedspreads worked in yellow linen thread and household linen worked in chain stitch on net and cambric.

Nisa embroidery on bridal linen and towel ends may be mistaken for lace, which is in fact used to finish the edge. Simple shapes are outlined with narrow buttonhole, closely worked; threads cut and withdrawn from the background are ornamented with various fillings, whipped and needlewoven with Greek cross between.

Madeira work is a type of whitework similar to *broderie anglaise*.

TURKEY

The two main styles of Turkish embroidery—floral patterns on cotton or fine linen and heavy gold on velvet—spread over a wide area. Early square cloths, turban covers, all have a circular design in the centre with flower sprays springing from it, mingling with other flowers in each corner.

Any article not in use is covered with a cloth and the greater the value of the article the more rich the embroidery on the cover. Towels are embroidered with floral sprays of carnation, hyacinth, pomegranate, rose and peony in pastel colours, arranged in spot patterns or in rows along a border.

Greek peasant costume, from the Keratia district, 19th century.

The stitch most used is double darning; closed buttonhole, whipped satin, encroaching satin, chained border, four-sided stitch, stem stitch used as a close filling and three-sided Turkish stitch are also worked—all having the advantage of being more or less reversible. On many towels only close inspection reveals the right side. The Turkish cavalry was richly equipped with embroidered velvet and leather harness.

Weapon sheaths and handles were embroidered in silk and metal thread or fine gold and silver wire. Tents were decorated with cloth and linen appliqué, a tradition still alive in the Middle East today.

GREECE

Embroidery of mainland Greece, unlike that of the islands, is Balkan in character, inclining towards Turkish or Slavonic according to locality. In general, where Turkish influence is strong more gold and silver thread is used on costume and in Slavonic regions more cross stitch. In the Epirus, the part of Greece most distant from Turkey, a minor school of embroidery flourished in the late 18th and early 19th centuries which showed much Islamic influence and included many slightly adapted Islamic motifs. In Metsovo, east of this region, the women wear a very handsome Sunday costume. Hems of full-length dresses, embroidered with a wide border of scrolling gold thread or bright silk flowers, are in strong colours which hold their own against the black sleeveless coats edged with wide, brilliant red bands.

Other interesting regional peasant costumes come from Kymi on Euboea, and Astypalea. Women of Kymi wear a full-sleeve jacket in Turkish style with bands of gold, a silk embroidered forehead cloth and long, white scarf with embroidered ends.

In Astypalea the most important part of a woman's dress, the sleeves, are embroidered in threaded chevron, and the skirt in cross stitch. In this case different types of traditional design are used together, a geometric pattern known as the Dixos on the sleeves with dragons and ships on the skirt hem.

Crete

Crete developed its own style with ideas assimilated from Byzantium, Italy and Turkey during successive periods of occupation. The most spectacular designs are on the wide borders of women's skirts, embroidered in a variety of bright shades of floss silk. Carnation sprays, roses, the Tree of Life, the Byzantine two-headed eagle and a curious double-tailed mermaid are among the motifs used. Cretan feather occurs more than any other stitch, worked closely without an outline. Other stitches include satin, herringbone, chain, French knots, ladder, fishbone, stem and whipped overcast.

On scarves, which need to be reversible since they hang down over the shoulder, double running and satin stitches are used too. A sharp acid yellow colour and black are very representative of Cretan work.

Other Greek islands

The Dodecanese. In the 18th century Patmos, Cos and Rhodes specialised in linen bed curtains. In Rhodes and Cos

Red waistcoat, embroidered in Paisley pattern, about 1840.

these developed into circular tents embroidered over the whole area. Formal patterns in darning, satin and chain stitch were arranged in stripes over the main surface; only at the apex of the opening was a divergence allowed. Here were animals and birds, flowers, ships and people and here a greater variety of stitches and colours, in contrast to the brick red and green silk elsewhere. In the work of Cos, cross stitch predominates; in Rhodes, influenced by Europe, small cross or stem stitches were worked in very thick untwisted silk on heavy linen, producing a rough nubbly effect.

The Cyclades. 17th-century bed curtains and valances are worked in fine patterned darning on linen, chiefly in red silk, although brown and green are known. Formal geometric leaf and star designs cover large areas. Traditional motifs include an irregular hexagon (the king pattern) and diamond (queen) which were used in many different ways to form patterns.

Ionian Islands. Here developed two styles for bed furnishings. One is influenced partly by Italian design, using cross stitch with a drawn-thread background of whipped stitch, the stylised birds, deer and flowers worked in red, green, blue and yellow. The second style is in split stitch and darning, with people in Turkish costume, surrounded by Turkish flowers, birds and the two-headed eagle.

Northern Sporades. Work in silk on linen is gay and spontaneous. The best-known motif, from Skyros, is a bird called either cock or peacock which sprouts flowers and leaves from feet and tail. Sometimes the shoulders even support a tall tulip stem dressed with tiny sprigs. Red, blue, brown, yellow and white, or blue, green, rust, ochre and white are often found together, a wider range of colours than on most Greek embroidery. Another typical design is of a ship, deck and rigging crowded with passengers and Cyclopean crew, one eye apiece, escorted by fish, while birds, sun-discs, flowers and people gambol in the sky above. Stitches include double darning, patterned darning, satin and counted satin, stem and oriental.

CYPRUS

Cyprus white embroidery was probably known before the Venetian occupation in the 16th century. A style called Levkara, strongly influenced by Italian design and stitchery, involves geometric satin, four-sided stitch, eyelet holes, cut squares with narrow woven bars and picots and needlewoven hems, worked on linen. Levkara work, of a high technical standard, is now known as Cyprus embroidery.

HUNGARY

Hungary has been influenced by Byzantium, the Italian Renaissance and Turkey during its occupation. In spite of unrest a national style arose. Embroidery on linen clothes and household linen had more effect on the country than the large amounts of metal thread used in Turkish embroidery on costume. Hungarian embroiderers rejected much of Italian Renaissance design, keeping a symmetrical floral arrangement to which was added Turkish and Persian motifs—rose, pomegranate, daisy and carnation joining the tipped pine cone of Kashmir, which changed into a small curved leaf.

Many different techniques were in use: surface stitchery in silk and metal thread; whitework in silk and linen thread using drawn-thread fillings, hem stitch, geometric satin and button-hole rings; *point de Hongrie* worked on oriental motifs in Renaissance style, the areas of stitchery unusually small; counted satin in diverse small patterns outlined with stem stitch; metal thread on velvet and applied motifs with metal thread; silk fabric entirely covered with couched metal thread in basket, chevron and other patterns.

Household linen varies less than costume from one district to another. Pillow decoration is essentially Hungarian: pillow ends generally have a wide border edged by narrower ones. Women's shifts, men's shirts, kerchiefs, coifs and aprons were embroidered on the counted thread, using cross and long-armed cross, diagonal chained border, counted satin, needle-woven borders and drawn-thread work. Free embroidery design sometimes had symmetrical plants with pine cone leaves, pomegranates, carnations and a long trailing leaf. Some designs reflect Turkish gold designs but are worked instead in a thick white thread.

The furriers and Szür makers were guilds of craftsmen. The furriers tailored cloaks, jackets and waistcoats of sheepskin and embroidered their own work. The 'suba', a full-length cloak, was made of fourteen skins arranged in a circle with floral embroidery at top and bottom of each seam, the composite motif at the bottom known as a 'rose'. The 'kodmon', a jacket worn by men and women, had embroidery over most of the back, on the front and shoulders. Appliqué in coloured leather was later combined with, then superseded by, embroidery. The Szür makers tailored frieze, a heavy material woven from the coarse wool of Hungarian sheep, bleached white.

Embroidery on frieze mantles increased until there were five silk floral bands on the side panels and other motifs on collar, sleeves, centre back, front panels and hem. These were made up of the rose, carnation, tulip, pomegranate, buds and small leaves. Patterned edges of applied frieze were held with closely stitched wool couching. Motifs and background between them were completely filled in with satin or flat stitch in crewel wool.

Certain stitches differ from those of the rest of Europe: double darning, double stitch, heavy chain, figure-of-eight stitch and enclosed herringbone.

ROUMANIA

Peasant designs show a certain unity in spite of wide regional variation, for instance the parts of the costume chosen for embroidery are usually the same and geometric designs predominate. In the north-east contact with the Ukraine and Russia affect both design and colour. Near the Danube Turkish costume and use of gold on velvet prevail and in another area Hungarian styles are found.

Collar from Dubrovnik, Yugoslavia.

The blouse is always beautifully embroidered, with wide horizontal bands, vertically striped sleeves, patterned bodice, neckband and hems. Generally geometric, these patterns are worked in coloured cotton or wool, occasionally with some silver thread, in cross stitch, darning, satin and geometric satin and eyelets. Perhaps most decorative of all work is the costumes of the Transylvanian Saxon people. On their summer clothes star designs in cross stitch and darning are unusually elaborate; floral designs and animals also appear.

Floral-patterned bonnets are worn and hems can be edged with lace or a large-holed type of *broderie anglaise*. In Calata a long, wide cotton napkin embroidered all over with flowers is the distinctive feature.

Yugoslavian mat worked in long-armed cross and Holbein stitches.

YUGOSLAVIA

Designs are generally geometric, with formalised flowers and animals. Wool from the black sheep is common in the south and Slovenia, but usually the thread used is made from unwashed fleece; it is very hard and thin and almost indestructable. Red is the dominant colour of the Slavs in the south and indigo of the Dalmatians; other colours might be yellow, blue or reddish-brown. Material is usually bleached or natural linen, or hemp in the north, though the Turkish influence in Montenegro brought richer fabrics—pale blue cloth and purple, mauve and black velvet. Each district uses one basis stitch, supplemented by others. For geometric designs this might be slanting Slav, chain or cross stitch, sometimes with darning and satin stitches.

Opposite: Roumanian peasant costume, 19th century. Embroidery is in coloured silks, and copper-gilt and silvered copper strips.

Tools and equipment

The following gives a list of the basic equipment required for embroidery. No doubt as your work progresses, and you become more ambitious, you will find other accessories which are helpful to you, but for the moment this list gives only the basic essentials which every needlewoman should have.

Needles

Crewel needles are long and sharp with a long eye. They are used with most embroidery threads.

Chenille needles are slightly shorter than crewel with a long wide eye. Chenilles are suitable for use with wool, and are also useful for thicker threads on surface embroidery and for taking ends of couched threads through fabric.

Tapestry needles have a rounded point and a thick eye and are used for embroidery on canvas or net and for counted-thread work on coarse linen.

Sharp needles are used for plain sewing.

If your workbox contains the following you will have a good selection, but turn to the chart on page 47 for exact details of which needle to use with which thread and fabric.

No. 8 sharp needle for plain sewing and embroidery with fine thread.

No. 7 crewel needle for surface embroidery in *coton à broder*, 2 or 3 strands of stranded cotton and 1 thread of crewel wool.

No. 5 crewel needle for heavier threads.

No. 24 tapestry needle for drawn-fabric work and canvas embroidery.

No. 22 tapestry needle for tapestry wool on canvas.

From right to left: No. 8 sharp needle with one thread of stranded cotton; No. 7 crewel needle with several threads of stranded cotton; No. 22 tapestry needle with crewel wool; No. 18 tapestry needle with rug wool; chenille needle with soft embroidery thread.

Thimble

Use on the middle finger of the hand which holds the needle. Metal thimbles are preferable to bone or plastic, but should be fairly light.

Stiletto

This is a needle screwed on to a handle, rather as a sewing-machine needle is attached. A stiletto is used to pierce material at the point where the thread is to enter, preparing the way for the needle actually carrying the thread. It is used on heavy materials like brocade and leather and is particularly useful when gold thread is being used as this is very liable to fray.

Scissors

It is a good idea to have two pairs—one medium-sized pair for cutting out fabric and a small, pointed pair for cutting threads.

Threads

In addition to the following special embroidery threads it is useful to have tacking cotton, No. 40 mercerised cotton in black and white and a selection of colours, plus oddments of yarn such as mohair and slub knitting yarn.

Stranded cotton has six strands loosely twisted together. It unravels easily so you can use as many or as few strands as you like. It is suitable for most types of embroidery.

Coton à broder is a highly twisted, lustrous thread. It is suitable for drawn-thread work, drawn-fabric work and cutwork.

Soft embroidery thread has a thick matt finish. It is suitable for bold free-style embroidery and counted-thread work.

Pearl cotton No. 5 and No. 8 are smooth corded threads. They are most suitable for Hardanger and other types of counted-thread work.

Tapestry wool is a firm, well-twisted woollen yarn. It is suitable for canvas embroidery as well as free-style and counted-thread work.

Metal threads—mainly gold and silver—come in several different textures and thicknesses.

Beads

A box of beads, sequins, press studs, hooks and eyes and other oddments is a good stand-by.

Iron, ironing board and pressing cloth

As well as pressing the finished embroidery, it is a good idea to give it a press occasionally as it is being worked. Press face downwards on a well-padded board. An iron is also needed for transferring purchased transfers to fabric.

Sewing machine

If you have a machine you can work machine embroideries (see page 102), but a sewing machine is also useful for making up hand embroideries into cushions and other items.

Frames

There are two types of frame, the round tambour frame and

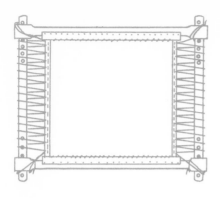

the rectangular slate frame. Details of these are given below.

You will also need . . .

Dressmaker's steel pins, lillikins (very tiny pins), pincushion, tape measure, pencils, paints, fine brush, paper, tracing paper, paste and powdered charcoal for pounce—for transferring designs (see page 51).

FRAMES

Small pieces of linen embroidery can be worked without mounting them in a frame first. However, if the work has complicated stitches or has areas of closely worked stitches it is best to use a frame or you may find your embroidery beginning to pucker.

The most common—and easiest type of frame to use—is the tambour or Swiss embroidery frame. This consists of two hoops, one slightly larger than the other. The fabric is placed over the smaller of the two hoops and then the larger hoop is placed over the smaller, thus holding the fabric tight. Some of the large tambour frames have a screw on the larger hoop which is tightened after the hoop has been placed over the fabric. This allows fabric of any thickness to be used. Sometimes the frame has a clamp so it can be fixed to the table or is attached to a wooden base so it can be held on the knee. If you are using a tambour frame for a large piece of embroidery, it is advisable not to keep the frame over the same part of the fabric for too long. A piece of muslin between hoops and fabric is a good idea, too, to protect the fabric.

For large pieces of work a square or rectangular frame, sometimes known as a slate frame, is best. This consists of two horizontal bars, each with tape nailed along it. The fabric to be embroidered is stitched to the tape on the bars with oversewing. Two side strips which slot into the bars are then screwed in place so the material is being held taut. The fabric is then attached to the side strips: thick material or canvas can be laced to the strips directly; fine material must first have tape sewn to its edge and the tape laced to the side strips.

Below, right: a tambour or Swiss embroidery frame.
Below, left: a 19th-century table slate frame.

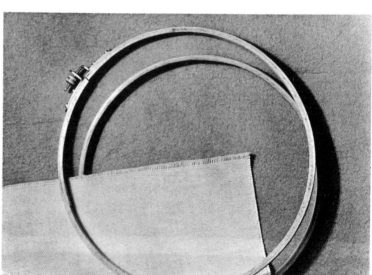

FABRIC	THREAD	NEEDLE
TRACED OR TRANSFERRED DESIGNS		
Fine linen, lawn, organdie, sheer silk or fine synthetics	Stranded cotton—1, 2 or 3 strands Pearl cotton No. 8 *Coton à broder* No. 18	Crewel No. 8 for 1 or 2 strands; No. 7 for 3 Crewel No. 6 Crewel No. 7
Medium-weight linen, rayon, sail cloth, satin, etc.	Stranded cotton—2, 3 or 4 strands Pearl cotton No. 8 *Coton à broder* No. 18	Crewel No. 8 for 2 strands; No. 7 for 3; No. 6 for 4 Crewel No. 6 Crewel No. 7
Heavy linen, crash or furnishing fabrics	Stranded cotton—6 strands Pearl cotton No. 5 Soft embroidery Tapestry wool	Crewel No. 5 Crewel No. 5 Chenille No. 19 Chenille No. 19
COUNTED-THREAD WORK		
Fine even-weave linen	Stranded cotton—1 to 6 strands Pearl cotton No. 8 or No. 5 *Coton à broder* No. 18	Tapestry No. 25 for 1 or 2 strands; No. 24 for 3; No. 23 for 4; No. 21 for 6 Tapestry No. 23 for No. 8; No. 21 for No. 5 Tapestry No. 24
Medium-weight even-weave linen	Stranded cotton—3, 4 or 6 strands Pearl cotton No. 8 or No. 5 *Coton à broder* No. 18 Tapestry wool	Tapestry No. 24 for 3 strands; No. 23 for 4; No. 21 for 6 Tapestry No. 23 for No. 8; No. 21 for No. 5 Tapestry No. 24 Tapestry No. 19
Coarse even-weave linen and fabrics	Stranded cotton—4 or 6 strands Pearl cotton No. 5 Soft embroidery Tapestry wool	Tapestry No. 23 for 4 strands; No. 21 for 6 Tapestry No. 21 Tapestry No. 19 Tapestry No. 19

Needles, threads and fabrics

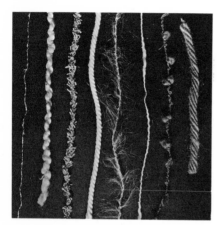

A selection of threads suitable for couching.

The correct combination of needle, thread and fabric is essential to achieve a good result in embroidery, and chart on page 47 will give you a guide to this. The more experienced embroiderer can tell by the feel of the needle and thread going through the fabric whether it is right or not. Individual preference does play a part, but remember that the needle should pierce the fabric easily and pull the thread through easily and the eye must be large enough to carry the thread smoothly. Heavy thread taken through a thin fabric may cause puckering, even if the eye of the needle makes a hole in the surface large enough for the thread to pass through easily. It also weakens the fabric.

NEEDLES

Always buy good-quality needles—they cost only a little more—and keep them in a flannel book, not a pincushion. Do not continue to use a needle if it has become crooked or worn—a crooked needle sews a crooked stitch and a needle with a worn eye will fray the embroidery thread.

THREADS

All embroidery threads are fairly loosely twisted—their purpose is to cover the material not to hold pieces together. Make sure that the thread stays twisted during work and if it does straighten out turn the needle a few times to retwist it. Move the position of the needle on the thread during work, so that the thread does not become worn in one particular place. Always cut threads; never try to break them. Have a good supply of each colour you are using as dye lots may vary slightly and you may not be able to get an exact match if you have to buy some more. If you are making an article you will want to wash often it is a good idea to match thread with fabric, using cotton thread on cotton, or linen on linen.

FABRICS

Always buy good-quality fabrics—it is foolish to waste time, thought and energy on a fabric which is not going to last. On the other hand do not buy too grand a fabric if you are a beginner as this will impose even greater stress on you to make your stitchery live up to the cloth. A good idea for a beginner is to practise the stitches on some inexpensive linen, then on a spare piece of the main fabric to get the feel of working on it. In this way you will be more certain of achieving a good final result. Even-weave linen is an excellent fabric to practise on as the threads can easily be counted and regular stitches learnt right from the start.

All fabrics can be embroidered in some form or another, and once you are acquainted with your stitches and a few types of embroidery it is easy to see the possibilities and scope for work which different materials offer. As a rule, simple embroideries work best on inexpensive materials and elaborate on more plush fabrics. If you wish to work a particular type of embroidery, then you should choose a fabric to suit it.

Working with linen

Linen is an excellent material for embroidery both for free-style and counted-thread work. Embroidery on linen never covers all the fabric, and nowadays linen is available in a variety of colours as well as white or unbleached. As you will probably want to wash an embroidery worked on linen, make sure you are using washable, colour-fast threads. For an article which is going to be washed a good deal, cotton or linen threads work best. Linen is also excellent for machine embroideries.

Working with silk and velvet

From earliest times embroidery has been worked on these two fabrics, both for church use and for elaborate domestic use. Buy the best silk you can afford, as thick as possible as thin fabric may stretch out of shape during work. Buy a short-pile velvet as stitches will be lost in a deep pile. Always mount the work in a strong frame, preferably lined with a firm linen first. Trace the design on by the pricking and pouncing method (see page 51) and use silk threads. The stitch most often used on silk and velvet is satin.

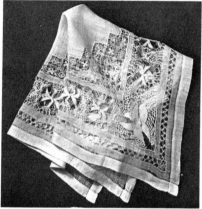

A fine handkerchief embroidered with Mexican hemstitch, late 19th century.

Working with fine fabrics

Fine fabrics include organdie, muslin, tulle, net and synthetics such as nylon and Terylene. Organdie has become increasingly popular as a material for embroidery and looks particularly good when the thread is the same colour as the material. It is generally advisable to use a frame for work on organdie. Stranded cotton is a suitable thread—select the number of strands according to the effect you want to create.

Tulle and net are hardwearing materials. A soft thread must be used with tulle—1, 2 or 3 strands of stranded cotton or machine embroidery cotton work well, or, for a coarser effect, *coton à broder* or pearl cotton.

Remember that good technique is needed for work upon fine fabrics and you must use a good thread. Methods most often used are satin stitch, *broderie anglaise*, shadow work and many kinds of drawn-fabric and drawn-thread work.

Shadow work is embroidered on either muslin or organdie. The work is always detailed, the design being worked in closed herringbone. This is most easily done from the back; it appears as double back stitch on the right side (see page 55). Since double back stitch will not lie flat if stretched across a wide area, designs are made of many small shapes or long curving lines. Pale material and light thread give the best result. Several colours are now often used and shadow work combined with surface stitchery. It should be remembered when choosing other stitches that all threads on both sides will show and thread ends must always be invisibly fastened off. Some surface stitches work very well—feather, fly and buttonhole are good

'Pharaoh', an impressive modern embroidery worked with gold threads, pearls and sequins.

examples—but buttonhole wheel, Cretan, stem, straight, Roumanian, chain, chained feather and back may also be used. Shadow work can be used for delicate table linen, dressing-table and other runners, baby dresses and dresses for small children, and baby pillows if worked on muslin.

Darning on net was very popular in the 19th century. Hexagonal net allows flexibility in design and many different fillings to be used. For this work the design is drawn on glazed linen and the net tacked over it to stay there until the work is finished. An outline, continuous if possible, is threaded with a line of running stitch either with a thick soft thread or with several strands so that ends of the outline and of the finer patterned darning threads can be hidden in it. Net can now be bought in many colours and different sizes of mesh. Embroidery need not be in the same colour but a shade of the same colour or one other colour only works best.

Working with gold thread

Gold thread is associated with ecclesiastical embroidery and work on silk, velvet and brocade. It can also be used on other firm fabrics and leather and is particularly good with blackwork, appliqué and collage. Only really experienced embroiderers should attempt ecclesiastical work with gold thread. Nowadays untarnishable metal threads are available in a variety of thicknesses. Japanese gold is made of gold leaf on tissue paper wound over a silk core.

Before working with gold thread, the fabric must be mounted in a frame to leave both hands free. The gold is laid on the fabric and sewn in place with small stitches in silk thread—yellow for gold and grey for silver. These stitches must be placed regularly and fairly close together. The ends of the gold have to be taken through to the back of the work by means of a large-eyed chenille needle. Other stitchery can become entangled with these ends so it is best to complete the embroidery and lay the gold as a final process. For thick fabrics it may be advisable to use a stiletto to make holes in the fabric for the gold thread (see page 45).

TRANSFERRING DESIGNS TO FABRIC
Purchased transfers

Transfers come in blue, yellow or black print. The yellow transfers are suitable for black material, the blue for light shades and the black for blue, green or brown material. Some are single impression transfers that can be used only once; some are multi-print which can be used up to eight times depending on the type and weight of fabric used (they last longer if used with fine fabrics).

First cut away all lettering from the transfer and keep aside to use for testing. Heat the iron to a fairly hot temperature (wool) for a single-impression transfer or hot (cotton) for a multiprint transfer. Lay the cut-away lettering shiny side downwards on a spare piece of fabric. Test the heat of the iron by applying it for a few seconds and then lifting the paper off. If the design has not transferred properly you need the iron a little hotter. Now place the main transfer sheet shiny side downwards on the main fabric in the required position and secure with pins. Apply iron for a few seconds and remove. Check that the design has transferred properly this time by lifting a corner; if it has not reapply the iron for a few seconds. Now carefully peel off paper—if it sticks to the fabric run the iron over it again. Take care not to move transfer or fabric or the impression will smudge.

If you are using a very rough or coarse material, immediately before transferring the design press the fabric with a hot iron over a damp cloth. This will flatten the surface temporarily. Lay the transfer on quickly and keep the iron on the transfer for longer than with a normal fabric. If the transfer still appears faint, paint over it with a fine brush and waterproof ink.

Tacking to tissue paper

This method is possible when the design is fairly simple. It can be used on almost any fabric and is particularly useful for fabrics such as towelling when the prick and pounce method (see below) is not possible.

Trace the design on to tissue paper, then place the tissue paper over the fabric. Tack along the lines of the design with $\frac{1}{4}$-in. stitches. Remove the tissue, scratching under each stitch to release the paper. If done carefully the paper can be lifted off in one piece. Do not rip the paper off in any case, as this could harm the fabric. Tack with thread of a similar colour to the material as this will not affect the colour scheme while work progresses. Remove tacking stitches immediately they have served their purpose.

Pouncing

When a design is too complicated to be tacked through tissue paper on to the material, this method provides the only accurate way to transfer a detailed design. Sixteenth and 17th-century embroidery pattern books contain pricked pages, although the method was probably known long before then.

Trace the design on to paper then place the tracing on a pad of spare material. Using a needle, prick holes along every line, making the pricks about $\frac{1}{10}$ in. apart. Do not use a pin as it makes too large a hole. On a long curving line you can make the holes in pairs and leave a larger gap between each pair.

Pin the material to be embroidered on to a drawing board, then lay the pricked paper over it. It is very important that the material does not move until the whole process is complete. Make sure that the paper will not be in a draught. Make a tight roll of spare fabric, about the size of a finger. Dip the end of the roll into powdered charcoal (pounce) for a light-coloured material or powdered cuttlefish or French chalk for a dark-coloured material. Shake off any excess. Dab roll on to the tracing, making sure that just enough falls through the holes to leave a clear line of dots beneath. Gently lift away the tracing paper without disturbing the fabric beneath.

Join the dots together with a very fine brush held vertically and water-colour paint, only just damp enough to make a hair line. When completed, shake fabric to remove pounce.

Transferring to canvas

Draw the design on to paper with a heavy outline. Place paper under canvas and trace it through, using paint or Indian ink. Pencil will not work because it smudges and disappears.

Transferring to a transparent fabric

Draw the design on paper with a clear enough line to show through the fabric. Place material over design then trace it on to the fabric using either a 2H pencil (which is hard enough not to crumble) or a fine brush and paint, making a very fine line.

For net, draw the design on glazed linen. Tack the net over it and leave the linen in position until the work is finished.

Waxed carbon paper

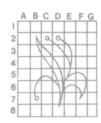

Use yellow or light blue carbon paper for dark-coloured fabrics, black or dark blue carbon for light-coloured fabrics. Place carbon paper shiny side downwards on the fabric, then place the design on top. Draw over all lines with a pencil with a sharp point.

This method is not nearly so satisfactory as any of the others. If you do attempt it, use fairly worn-out carbon paper—never use a tracing wheel as this is very hard to manipulate and is useless for reproducing any detail.

REDUCING OR ENLARGING A DESIGN

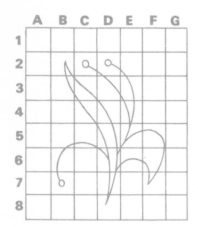

Take your paper with the design on it and divide it into squares with ruler and pencil. If you do not want to mark the drawing of the design, put a sheet of tracing paper over the top and divide this up into squares. Now number the squares along the top and down the side. Take another piece of paper and mark squares on this, either larger or smaller than the original as you require.

For instance, if you want the design twice the size of the original, you should divide the original into $\frac{1}{2}$-in. squares and the second piece of paper into 1-in. squares. Number the squares the same as for the original design. You can now sketch in the design, first marking the points where the design crosses the lines of the squares, then joining these points, following the original design.

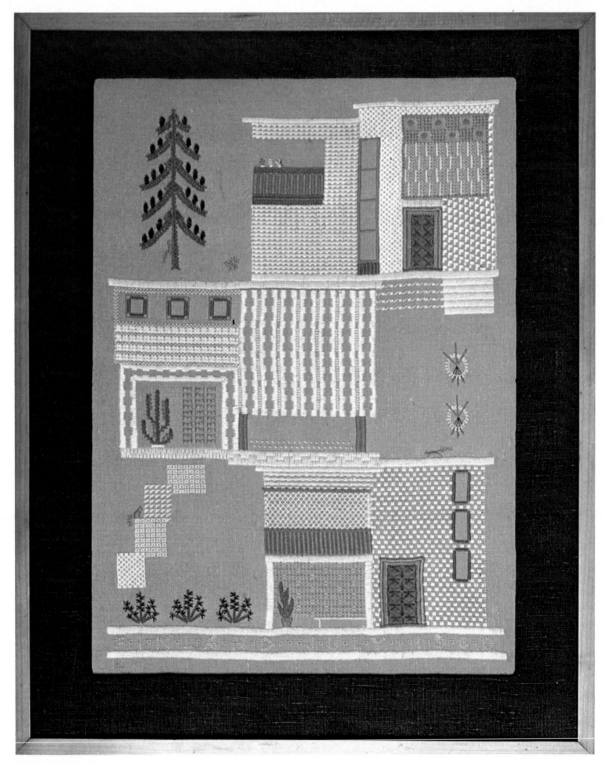

'Houses in Finland', a counted-thread sampler on linen.

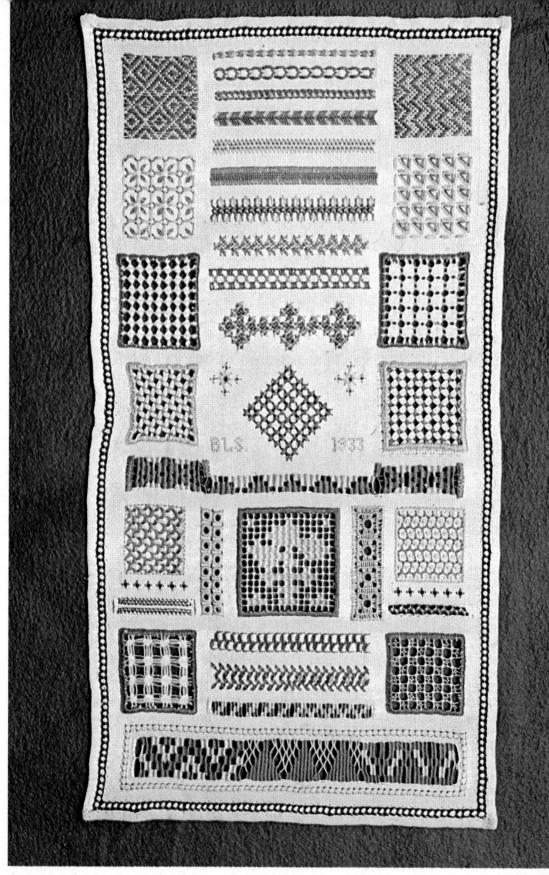

A sampler of various counted and drawn-thread stitches.

Free embroidery stitches

BACK
This makes the narrowest line of all embroidery stitches.

Work from right to left. Bring needle through on stitch line, insert it a short step back and bring it out again at an equal distance in front of starting point. Repeat along line.

Threaded (or laced) back stitch
The wave line is more effective if worked in a different thickness of thread. If threaded once in each direction, a series of small circles form.

Having worked a line of back stitch, bring needle through in centre of one stitch, then weave thread under stitches, first stitch from left to right, second from right to left, and so on to end, without needle entering fabric.

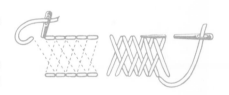

Double back stitch or closed herringbone stitch
When double back stitch is worked, closed herringbone stitch appears on the wrong side, and vice versa. You can therefore work from either side of work to achieve effect required.

Working as double back stitch: work small back stitches alternately along bottom stitch line and top stitch line. Working as closed herringbone: work herringbone stitch (see page 63) with no spaces between stitches.

Whipped back stitch
Having worked a line of back stitch, bring needle out at same place as one stitch then take thread over and under each back stitch without entering fabric.

BULLION KNOT
Groups of bullion knots can be used for flower centres and spot patterns. The stitch needs careful practice.

Bring needle out at top of length required for knot and make a back stitch to bottom of length required; bring needle only partly out at original point. Twist thread loosely round the top of needle, 6 or 8 times, or enough to make the right length of stitch. Hold carefully with left thumb while pulling needle through. Turn needle ready to insert at bottom of stitch, pull the thread tight and pass needle through to back.

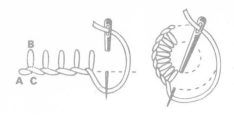

BUTTONHOLE AND BLANKET STITCHES

These are worked in the same way; the difference is that buttonhole stitches are worked close together while blanket stitches have space between them.

Work from left to right. Bring thread out on horizontal line (point A), insert at top of stitch (point B) and bring out again directly underneath on lower line (point C), holding thread under needle point. Repeat along line.

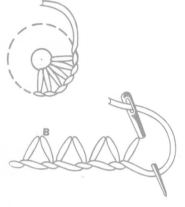

Buttonhole wheel

This is buttonhole stitch worked in a circle with the top of the stitches all going into the same point. A small hole should form in the centre.

Closed buttonhole stitch

Work in the same way as buttonhole stitch, but use point B as top of two consecutive stitches, so each pair of stitches forms a triangle.

Crossed buttonhole stitch

Work from left to right. Bring needle out at bottom of stitch at point A, insert at top of stitch and to the right at point B, bringing needle out again at point C on bottom line halfway between A and B and holding thread under needle. Now insert needle at D above C and bring out at E on bottom line underneath B, again holding thread under needle. Repeat.

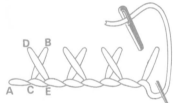

Knotted buttonhole stitch

This is buttonhole stitch with a knot at the top of each stitch.

Work from left to right. Bring needle out on bottom line at A. Make a loop from right to left over the left thumb, and slip it on to needle. With loop still on needle, insert needle at B, and bring out directly underneath at C, holding thread under point of needle. Continue in this way.

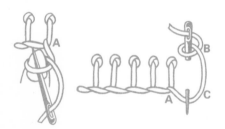

Spaced or grouped buttonhole stitch

This is buttonhole stitch worked in groups of 2 or 3, with the space between each group larger than that between each stitch.

CHAIN STITCH

Chain stitch makes a smooth-edged line which, particularly on curves, puckers quickly. This can be prevented if the fabric is curved over the finger, if only tiny pieces of fabric are picked up and if the stitch is kept fairly loose.

Bring needle out at top of stitch line. Holding thread down below stitch, insert needle again at top of stitch and bring it out again on stitch line above thread. Repeat along stitch line.

Cable chain stitch

The one disadvantage with this attractive stitch is that if a mistake is made the knot formed is difficult to unpick and the line may have to be cut out and started again.

Bring needle out at top of stitch line. Hold the thread down with your left thumb while the needle is twisted first under then over the thread. Insert needle into fabric at B and, still holding thread down, bring it up at C and pull through.

Chequered chain stitch

For this stitch the needle is threaded with 2 colours which are used alternately. Take care not to spoil the look of your embroidery; it is sometimes better to work 3 or 4 stitches in each colour at a time. When making each loop for chain stitch, hold one colour down with your thumb and let the other lie on top.

Detached chain stitch (sometimes known as daisy)

Work in the same way as chain stitch, but insert needle again just below thread to hold it down.

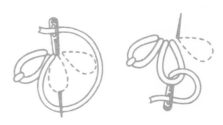

Double chain stitch

This is the same as closed feather stitch (see page 61).

Heavy chain stitch

This makes a wide line useful for outlining curved shapes in drawn-fabric work.

Bring needle through at top of stitch line and make a short stitch downwards. Bring needle up just below this stitch and pass the thread under the vertical stitch re-entering fabric at same place it came out. Bring needle out just below this and pass the needle under the vertical thread again. Continue making stitches in this way, passing needle under the two preceding loops.

Open chain stitch

Bring needle through at A, hold thread down with left thumb, insert needle at B and bring out at C, keeping thread loose. Holding thread down again, insert needle at D and bring out at E. Continue in this way.

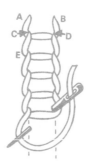

Rosette chain stitch

This stitch works particularly well on curved lines.

Work from right to left. Bring thread through at top of stitch, pass the thread over to the left side and hold down with the left thumb. Insert the needle a short distance to the left of where it originally came through and bring it out at bottom of stitch (A) with the thread under the needle point. Pass needle under top thread (B) without entering fabric. Continue to work in this way.

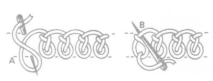

Russian chain stitch
Work a chain stitch in the usual way then work 2 detached chain stitches from it, one going to each side as shown in diagram.

Twisted chain stitch
Work as for chain stitch, but instead of needle entering fabric in the same place as it emerged, insert it to the left, across the thread.

Zig-zag cable chain stitch
Work as cable chain stitch, but instead of working in a straight line, slant the needle first to the left and then to the right.

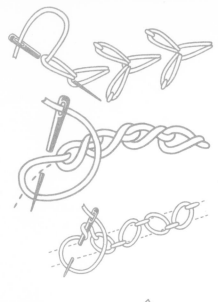

CHEVRON STITCH
This can be used as a line or as a filling. It is worked between two parallel lines.

Work from left to right. Bring needle up on lower line, insert a little to right and bring up again halfway between these 2 points. Insert needle on top line a little to right and bring out just to the left on the top line. Insert again on top line to right and bring out at centre of stitch on top line. Work in this way alternately on top and bottom lines.

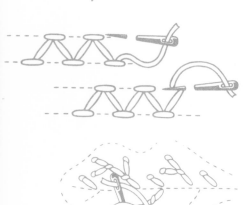

CORAL STITCH
Work from right to left. Bring thread out on stitch line, lay it along line and hold down with your left thumb. Take a small stitch under the line from top to bottom as shown in the diagram and pull through with the needle over the lower thread.

COUCHING
Couching is the method of sewing down a thick thread, bunch of threads, cord or gold with a thinner thread, preferably in a similar shade.

Lay the thread to be couched along the design line. Bring needle with couching thread through just beneath the design line and insert it just above, over the thread to be couched. Repeat at intervals, but not so close that couching thread spoils the effect of the thread being couched.

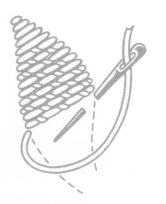

Bokhara couching
This stitch is used when laying thread to fill a space such as a leaf. The laid thread and the couching thread are the same and the couching stitches are arranged to form part of the pattern.

Bring thread out at left side of the space to be filled and carry it over the space to the right side. Bring needle up just below thread and a little to the left, take it over thread and insert above, then bring it out below thread again and a little further to the left. Continue along the line, then work the next row in the same way, making the couching threads fall in between those of the previous row as shown in the diagram.

Roumanian couching

This differs from Bokhara couching in that the couching thread makes a fairly long stitch across the laid thread as shown in the diagram. It is worked in the same way as Bokhara couching apart from this.

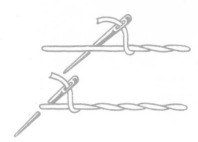

CRETAN STITCH

This is a versatile stitch which can be worked very closely to form a dense line, or openly to make a light filling. It can be placed in parallel rows or varied in length to fill a leaf or petal shape (see diagrams below).

Work from left to right. Bring needle through just above the centre of space being worked. With thread to the right, insert needle at bottom of space and bring up just below centre, with thread under needle. Still with thread to right, insert needle at top of space and bring out just above centre with thread under needle. Continue in this way.

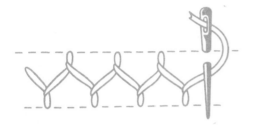

CROSS STITCH

Cross stitch should be worked only on the counted thread, and an even-weave material is essential. It should be used only with other counted-thread stitches. Stitches may be completed singly or worked in rows, the half of the stitch made from right to left being worked along the row and the cross from left to right being worked on the way back. The upper thread should always cross in the same way throughout the design unless change of texture is particularly required. As far as possible make only upright or horizontal stitches on the back (not diagonal).

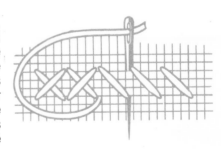

Bring needle through at lower right point of cross, take over to the top left point, bring through again at lower left point and take up to top right point. To work in rows, work from right to left for first half, working from lower right corner to top left for each cross; on way back work from lower left corner to top right for each cross.

Long-armed cross stitch or plaited Slav stitch

Work from left to right. Start at bottom left and work the longer part of the stitch to top right; now bring needle through below at bottom right and work up to top left, which is only halfway to the starting point. Bring needle up below to start next stitch.

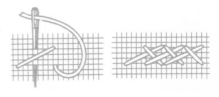

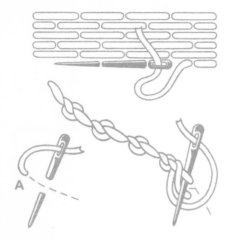

CROWN STITCH

Work as fly stitch (see page 62), then bring needle up in centre again and make a straight stitch each side of centre stitch the same length as centre stitch.

DARNING STITCH

Work from right to left. Bring needle through at end of line and make long stitches along line, taking only a very small piece of fabric each time. Work the row below in the same way, but with the stitches beginning in the centre of the stitches of the previous row as shown in diagram.

DOUBLE KNOT STITCH

Work from left to right. Bring needle through at A then make a small stitch at right angles to stitch line and pull through. Pass thread over then under stitch on surface without needle entering fabric. Now hold thread down with left thumb and pass the needle again over and under the stitch on surface. Pull thread through to make a knot. Space knots evenly and fairly closely for best effect.

FAGGOTING OR INSERTION STITCHES

A faggoting or insertion stitch joins together two finished edges. Before working the stitch tack the 2 edges on to glazed linen or a strip of smooth paper with just enough space between for the stitches.

Right: sampler of darning stitches on huckaback.
Far right: various insertion stitches.

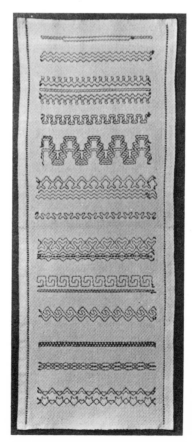

Buttonhole insertion stitch

This consists of groups of 4 buttonhole stitches (see page 56) worked alternately on each piece of fabric to be joined. Work the top row in the normal way and the bottom as shown in the diagram.

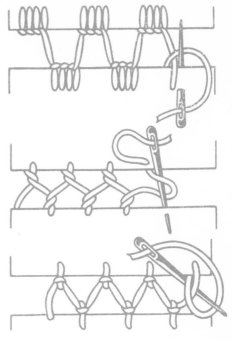

Faggoting or twisted insertion stitch

Work from left to right. Start from bottom edge, inserting needle from below a little way in from edge. Now insert needle into top edge from below, a little to the right. Twist needle under then over thread lying between the 2 edges, then insert needle into bottom edge from below, a little to the right. Continue working into each edge alternately twisting needle each time.

Knotted insertion stitch

Work from left to right. Insert needle from below on bottom edge, then holding thread to right insert needle into top edge from above. Now take needle behind both threads between edges and up with main thread below needle. Repeat on bottom edge, then alternately.

FEATHER STITCH

Start at top of stitch line and bring thread through. Holding thread down with left thumb, make a diagonal stitch, inserting needle to right of stitch line and bringing it out on stitch line a little below starting point and above thread. Now work in the same way but insert needle to the left of stitch line. Continue alternately in this way.

Chained feather stitch

Start at top, working down between two parallel lines. Bring thread through at left and make a chain stitch slanting towards the centre. Tie this down with a stitch about the same length as the chain, also slanting inwards. Bring needle out again at right side, just below bottom of chain stitch, and make another chain stitch, slanting towards centre. Tie this down in the same way as previous stitch. Continue in this way.

Closed feather stitch

Work from top to bottom. Bring needle out at left side, hold thread down with left thumb and insert needle at right side a little above starting point. Bring needle out on right side, a little below starting point, and with thread below needle. Now hold thread down again, insert needle at left side immediately below starting point and bring it out on left side, the stitch being the same length as before, with thread below needle. Repeat.

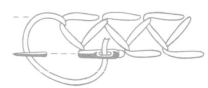

Double feather stitch

This is worked in the same way as feather stitch, except that 2 or more stitches are worked each side of the stitch line.

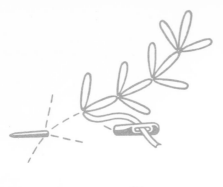

FERN STITCH

This stitch can become monotonous, but if the proportion of the centre and side stitches is changed it becomes more decorative. It can be used to hold down applied fabric.

Start just below top of stitch line. Make a straight stitch to the left, another to top of stitch line and another to right, bringing thread up after last stitch on stitch line a stitch length below starting point. Repeat.

FISHBONE STITCH

This can be used for a close border or for filling small shapes.

Bring thread through at side of shape to be filled and make a diagonal stitch to 2 threads beyond centre. Bring thread up at other side of shape and make a diagonal stitch to 2 threads beyond centre, so stitches overlap at centre. Repeat.

Open fishbone stitch

This is worked quite differently from fishbone stitch. Bring thread out just left of centre of shape and take it up to right edge diagonally. Bring needle out again on left edge of shape and take just to right of centre diagonally. Bring thread through again just to left of centre a little below, and repeat from beginning.

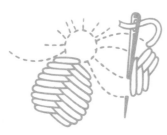

FLAT STITCH

This is worked in the same way as fishbone stitch, except that the stitches are worked horizontally, not diagonally, as shown in diagram.

FLY STITCH

This stitch can be worked horizontally from left to right, or vertically from top to bottom, or singly. It is like an open chain stitch.

Bring needle through at top left of stitch, hold thread down with left thumb, insert needle at top right of stitch and bring out at centre a little below, with thread below needle. If working horizontally tie down with a short vertical stitch over the thread, then bring needle through just to the right of the top right of stitch, ready for next stitch. If working vertically, tie down with a slightly longer vertical stitch, then bring needle up to left of middle of stitch, ready to continue.

FRENCH KNOT

Bring needle through where knot is required and hold thread firmly with finger and thumb of left hand. Twist needle twice round thread. Now still holding thread firmly, turn needle round to starting point and insert just behind it, gently pulling thread through. Beginners wrongly assume that a large French knot can be made by increasing the twists; however, the result is merely an unsightly mass of threads.

HERRINGBONE STITCH

Work from left to right. Bring needle out on lower line. Insert on top edge a little to right and take a small stitch backwards along top edge. Now insert on lower edge a little to right and take another small stitch to left. The fabric lifted by the needle and the space between the stitches should be the same to achieve best effect. Continue in this way.

Closed herringbone stitch
See double back stitch on page 55.

Threaded herringbone stitch
Work a row of herringbone stitch. Now lace through it, making small horizontal stitches over the crossed part of the herring-bone, with another colour of thread.

INTERLACED BAND

This stitch is not suitable for an article which will be washed frequently.

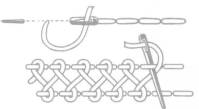

Work two parallel rows of back stitch (see page 55), with the ends of the stitches in one row level with the middle of the stitches of the other row. With a blunt needle and matching or contrasting thread, interlace top and bottom stitches alternately as shown in diagram.

LEAF STITCH

Start at bottom of shape. Bring needle through to left of centre and make a diagonal stitch to the right edge. Bring needle through to right of centre, level with starting point, and make a diagonal stitch to left edge. Bring thread up again to left of centre, just above starting point and continue in this way.

LOCK STITCH

First work a row of vertical straight stitches from right to left. Now work back, lacing thread through stitches as shown in diagram. Then lace the other side of the stitch in exactly the same way. The lacing thread can be a contrasting one, slightly thicker if liked.

This is generally used for shading in silk and crewel embroidery When worked perfectly in silk, no individual stitches show.

This is a variation of satin stitch (see page 65). In the first row satin stitches alternately long and short are used. In following rows stitches of even length are used to fill the spaces.

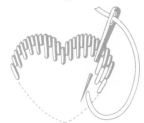

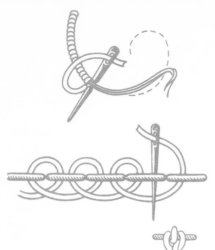

OVERCAST STITCH

This is used to protect the raw edge of eyelet holes, for monograms or for stalks or stems.

Bring needle through below stitch line, then work over line and bring needle through below line to the right. Repeat.

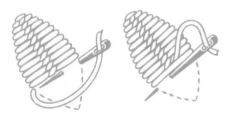

PEKINESE STITCH

Work a row of back stitch (see page 55). Interlace with a contrasting or toning thread as shown in diagram.

RAISED CHAIN BAND

Work a line of horizontal straight stitches, fairly close together. Start at top with a contrasting thread—the needle does not re-enter fabric after this. Pass thread over and under first bar coming out on left side. Holding thread down under needle, take needle over and under bar to the right of centre and pull through. Now repeat over next bar and so on.

ROUMANIAN STITCH

This stitch can often be substituted for satin stitch and gives a neater result. It is easier to achieve a smooth edge with this stitch, and little thread is wasted on the back.

Bring needle through at left edge of shape to be filled and insert it at right edge. With thread below needle bring needle through just to right of centre of shape. Take thread over long stitch, insert needle just to left of centre and bring it out again on left side of shape. Repeat.

RUNNING STITCH

This can be threaded or whipped as for back stitch (see page 55).

Work from right to left. Each stitch should be of equal length, crossing over 3 or 4 threads of fabric, but picking up only 1 or 2 threads in between.

Right: table mat in Holbein double running stitch. The edge is hemstitched and fringed.

Double running stitch or Holbein stitch
Work a row of running stitches, leaving the same number of threads between stitches as stitch length. Now work back with another row of running stitches, filling in the gaps left on the first row.

SATIN STITCH
Stitches must not be too long or they may pull out of shape. If liked, the shape can be padded with running stitches or felt.

Work straight stitches close together across the shape, carrying the thread behind the work between stitches.

Left: geometric satin stitch pincushion.

Surface satin stitch
This is an economical method of working satin stitch as all the thread is kept on the surface. Instead of carrying the thread behind the work, a tiny stitch of 1 or 2 threads is picked up and the thread carried over the surface to the other side.

SEEDING
This is a simple filling stitch composed of small scattered straight stitches of equal length.

SHEAF FILLING STITCH
This consists of 3 vertical satin stitches caught together in the middle with 1 or 2 overcast stitches. The overcast stitches are worked over only the satin stitches—the needle does not enter fabric. The stitch groups are placed alternately to make a chequered pattern.

SPANISH KNOTTED FEATHER STITCH
This is a quite difficult stitch to work until the rhythm has been discovered. Make sure that the needle points well outwards to leave sufficient room to work comfortably. Start at top of stitch line. Bring thread through and hold down to the left with your left thumb. Make a slanting stitch from right to left as shown in the diagram, bring needle out above working thread. Hold down to the right, then take a slanting stitch from left to right and pull through with needle over working thread as shown in diagram. Make another stitch to left, then another to right and so on, holding last loop down with a tiny stitch.

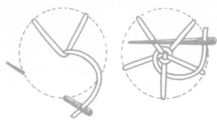

SPIDER'S WEB
Work a fly stitch (see page 62) with its centre in the centre of the circle to be filled, and caught down with a stitch to bottom of circle. Now work 2 straight stitches, one each side of last stitch, from edge of circle to centre, dividing circle into five as shown in diagram. Weave under and over stitches as shown until the circle is filled. In drawn-thread work only half the circle is filled.

SPLIT STITCH
This stitch should be worked with floss silk. Stitches should be very small.

Work from left to right. Bring needle through at end of stitch line, and make a small stitch over line, piercing the working thread with the needle as shown in the diagram.

STEM STITCH
This stitch can be used as a filling, with rows of stem stitch worked closely together, as well as an outline. Work from left to right. Bring needle through at end of line, then insert a little way to the right. Bring out again a little to the left, thus making a long step forward and a little one back. The thread should be kept below the needle.

'The Spinney', a modern embroidered panel incorporating simple stitchery, applied materials and beading.

Portuguese knotted stem stitch

Begin as for ordinary stem stitch. Now bring needle down and pass under stitch (not entering fabric), then pass needle under stitch again to left of first coil. Now work another stem stitch then pass needle twice under this and previous stitch together. Keep working in this way.

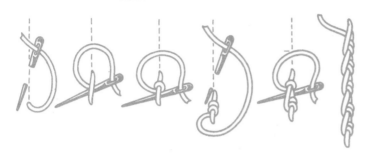

STRAIGHT STITCH

The stitches need not be all same length, but they should not be too long or too loose.

Bring needle out at beginning of stitch, insert at end and bring out again ready for next stitch.

VANDYKE STITCH

An even tension is important to prevent the central plait becoming untidy. Vandyke stitch makes a good band in a border design or it can be used as a ridged filling.

Work from top to bottom. Start at left edge below top of stitch line. Take thread up to top of stitch line at centre and take a tiny stitch from right to left at centre. Now make a long stitch to right edge, level with starting point, insert needle and carry thread across back bringing it out again on left edge just below starting point. Without needle entering fabric, take thread behind crossed threads in centre from right to left then insert needle on right edge just below previous point. Continue working in this way.

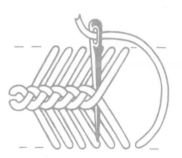

WHEATEAR STITCH

Work from top to bottom. Bring thread through on stitch line just below top. Make a diagonal straight stitch to left and another to right, bringing thread through again below starting point. Without needle entering fabric, take thread under the 2 straight stitches and insert at same place as before. Now make 2 more straight stitches and work along stitch line in this way.

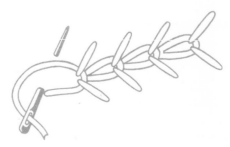

Lettering, alphabets and monograms

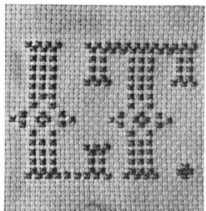

Examples of different styles of lettering. Top to bottom: cross stitch, Holbein double running, and eyelets with pulled satin stitch.

The use of initials for marking bed, table and personal linen dates back a long time. A piece of linen worked with signs and initials in brown thread belonging to the ancient Egyptians of the 14th century BC has been found. The Bayeux tapestry, as well as telling the story of the Battle of Hastings in pictures, has a brief commentary in clearly drawn capital letters.

Late 17th-century linen samplers included whole alphabets in different techniques—cross stitch, star and rococo stitches are some—and bands of letters in drawn-thread work or Italian needlepoint. Late 18th-century and 19th-century samplers made a feature of cross-stitch poems, texts, and alphabets as well as name, date and sometimes age of the embroiderer. A cloth in fine cross stitch has a border made entirely from the names of stations passed through during numerous train journeys. Another modern piece, a cloth in shadow work on organdie designed as a silver wedding gift, bears the names of the parents and their six children.

Lettering should be well formed, in good proportion and carefully spaced. Measurements between letters can never be used because each letter reacts to its neighbours. The only thing to do is plan carefully before starting to work. Each fabric to some extent dictates the style of lettering used upon it; for example in counted-thread work, in cross stitch, a minimum of seven blocks is needed for the height of each letter.

For initials you can use a single letter or two or more initials close together or interwoven. If they are interwoven one letter can be in a heavier stitch than the other. A cipher is two letters arranged ornamentally over each other and a monogram is two letters, the upright stroke of one letter also being the upright stroke of the other, so neither is quite complete. Transfers are available of single letters in different styles, or you can probably find letters to trace in books.

Initials can add much to household linen whether sheets, pillow cases, or tablecloths and give a little extra to lingerie, handkerchiefs, bags, blouses, belts and scarves as well. Almost any stitch can be used, but it is best to keep to fairly simple work for articles which are going to get a lot of wear. Cross stitch is often used on household linen. It is advisable to use a frame for lettering, particularly when a fine fabric which is likely to pucker is being used: a Swiss frame is best. Suitable threads are *coton à broder*, stranded cotton, and pearl cotton.

SIMPLE METHODS FOR LETTERING
Modern initials usually work best if they are fairly small and have an uncomplicated outline.

Letters can be worked in chain stitch, cross stitch, double back stitch or stem stitch or stem and double back combined.

The finer the cotton used, the smaller and more regular the stitches, the better the effect of chain stitch, particularly if coloured cotton is used. Corded outlines worked in *coton à broder*, stranded cotton or pearl cotton look very neat.

Cording
The cording thread should be quite thick and well twisted. Place the cording thread along the line to be worked and then with your top thread work vertical oversewing stitches over it so that it is completely covered. You can work from right to left or left to right as you prefer.

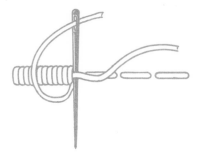

MORE ELABORATE METHODS FOR LETTERING
The cording mentioned above can be used for outlines with filling stitches of satin-stitch dots or alternating back stitches to make a more elaborate letter. Another idea is to work the outline in two rows of stem stitch, then fill the inner space with small darned wheels.

Padded satin stitch
This is probably the best-known type of lettering for initials and monograms. It works best with an old style of letter.

First outline the thick parts of each letter with fine running or chain stitches. Pad between these lines with chain stitch: first work round just inside the outline with the padding stitches, then continue round and round until the centre is reached. If you want your letter very embossed, work a second layer of chain over the first. Now cover with satin stitches, all slanting in the same direction. Crochet cotton makes a good padding with the satin stitch worked in linen or cotton thread.

Below: padded satin stitch; eyelets and four-sided stitch.

Cutwork
Cutwork gives a luxurious look to your lettering and is fairly easy to work, but the design must be planned properly in advance so no part of the letter is left unattached when the background is cut away. There is a chapter on cutwork beginning on page 85.

Outline the design with running stitch, working any necessary bars (see page 87) at the same time. Pad and cover letters with satin stitch as directed for padded satin stitch letters. When all is done cut background fabric away. This method is not really suitable for fabrics which are going to be washed a lot as it is rather fragile. If very delicate fabric is being worked, first back it with organdie and trim away afterwards.

Satin stitch can be combined with seeding or overcast stitch for letters. Thick parts of the letter are worked in satin stitch, while the narrow parts are worked in overcast. Two different colours of thread can also be used. Long-and-short stitch could be used instead of satin stitch as well.

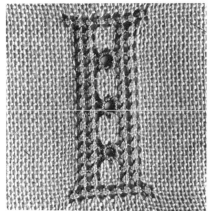

Using beads and sequins

Beads have been used for decoration ever since primitive man found the first stone with a naturally worn hole. Glass beads and pearls from European river shellfish were used in very early times. The first manufactured glass beads came from Venice and Murano, and later from Bohemia, which became the main sources for the Victorians. They decorated everything with beads: bags, belts, hats and dresses, as well as using them for fringes, pictures, frames and lampshades.

From Byzantine times onwards pearls and beads have been sewn on to dress and precious articles and on to church vestments. In Russia pearls played an important part in the elaborate headdresses once worn with traditional costume, and beads adorn many peasant costumes from Lapland southwards through central Europe to Hungary. In the 17th century Stuart pictures and caskets had animals and birds with bead eyes in otherwise pure silk embroidery. Stuart bead baskets were greatly treasured.

About 1854 large cylindrical beads were imported into England as well as 'pound' beads, in three sizes, sold by weight. The middle size was used on canvas for cushions, stool tops and table covers, often in conjunction with Berlin woolwork. Very small beads were sewn on net, making dainty purses and

Beadwork bag worked by Mary II, 1688.

Modern embroidered cushion covers.
Left: Kew, Penelope Design P533.
Above: Elke (top cover) and Inga,
Penelope Designs P412 and 410.
Below: Tivole, Penelope Design P397.

An example of shadow work.

necklets. Beads still appear on contemporary couture evening dresses, robes and evening bags, and are always kept handy by embroiderers.

Beads can be made of many materials, including steel and porcelain, though most often they are made of glass. They can be many shapes, regular and irregular, and a multitude of colours, both transparent and opaque. Sequins are small, shiny, flat circles with holes in the centres. They are very light and sparkling and come in black, white, mother-of-pearl, silver, gold and many iridescent colours.

A good strong thread is required for sewing on beads, as the sides of the hole in the bead may wear the thread away. *Coton à broder* is suitable and you can use it double if you think it will be necessary. Sometimes the hole in the bead is so small that only a very fine needle, with a hole not large enough to carry the thread you want to use, will go through it. In this case thread the needle with some fine strong thread and pull it through hole, leaving end of thread the other side of bead. Thread needle back again through hole, leaving a loop behind. Place the thread you want to use to hold the beads through the loop. Now pull the loop through the bead—the loop pulls the thread after it.

ATTACHING BEADS
Individually
Bring needle through fabric at place where bead is to go. Thread a bead on to needle and let it drop on to fabric. Now insert needle into fabric just next to place it came out. Bring needle up in right position for next stitch or bead.

In lengths
Attach end of thread which will hold beads to beginning of

Another modern embroidery showing the Three Kings (see also page 36), using applied materials, simple stitchery and beads and sequins.

Gold fabric, gold thread and tiny sparkling sequins and stones converted an ordinary cigar box into this rich-looking jewellery case.

design line. String required number of beads on thread. Move first bead to its right place on fabric, then with needle and another thread make a small stitch over bead thread immediately after bead. Put next bead in place and repeat.

By tambour stitch

For this you need a special hook, similar to a crochet hook. Trace design on wrong side of fabric and place fabric in a frame that will leave both hands free, with wrong side of fabric uppermost. Attach a long thread to wrong side of fabric then take it through to right side and hold it with the left hand underneath frame. String beads on to thread. Push hook through fabric from top and bring through thread from below to form a chain stitch. With left hand put a bead into place on right side, then push hook through again and pick up thread after bead and pull through to top. Continue working in this way.

ATTACHING SEQUINS

Overlapped

This is the most usual method. The sequins are sewn on with a back stitch.

Work from right to left. Bring needle through fabric on design line, the length of a sequin from end. Place sequin in position so right edge is at end of design line and hold in place with thumb. Insert needle through hole in sequin from top and into fabric, as shown in diagram, and bring out again on design line the length of a sequin from centre of first sequin. Place second sequin on fabric, with half of it overlapping first sequin and sew in place in same way as before. Continue along line.

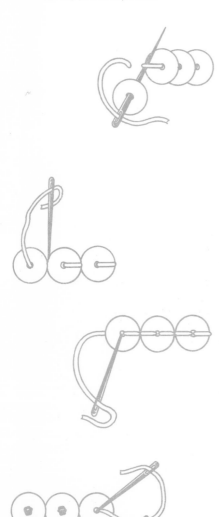

Individually

This method has a stitch going across half of sequin. Work from right to left. Bring needle through fabric on design line, a little way in from end. Thread sequin on to needle then hold in place on fabric with thumb. Take needle back across sequin and into fabric, then bring it out again along line to left, so that when next sequin is threaded on it will lie edge to edge with first sequin. Repeat along line.

With a decorative stitch

In this method the stitching goes right across sequins so it forms part of the pattern.

Start as for previous method, but bring needle out again at left edge of first sequin then work back through hole of sequin. Continue working twice into centre of each sequin in this way.

With a bead

No thread shows over sequin with this method as sequin is held in place by the bead.

Bring needle through fabric at place where centre of sequin is to go. String sequin on thread, then string on a small bead. Take needle back through hole in sequin and through fabric. Bring it out in position to work next sequin.

The importance of design

An embroidery you have designed yourself gives far more satisfaction than one you have worked from a transfer, and to do your own designing you do not have to be marvellous at drawing or full of original ideas—you can get inspiration from a number of sources. The three things that contribute most towards a really good piece of embroidery are even stitches, good colour scheme and an attractive arrangement of the design.

If you are a beginner and nervous of making your own designs, you can always start with some transfers. You could cut part of a transfer out and use it on some article for which the whole transfer was not intended, or you could take two or more transfers and borrow pieces from each to make your own design. Both of these are more personal than using a transfer just as it is, and if an effort has been made to use a transfer in an original way, then that is a form of designing. Another idea is to take a printed fabric, silk or brocade and embroider over part of its pattern. This works well if the material is made up into a dress, for instance. You can embroider just the sleeves, perhaps outlining the pattern with running stitch using a different shade or a contrasting colour. This gives the dress a very original look.

If you are going to design your own embroidery right from

The same motif worked in a variety of techniques. Top row, left to right: canvas work, cutwork, shadow work. Bottom row, left to right: Assisi work, cross stitch, Holbein double running, surface stitches.
In centre: appliqué.

Tea cosy worked in simple counted-thread stitches.

scratch here are some hints on how to set about it. First decide the article you are going to make, possibly a cushion or a tray cloth. It's best to choose something not too large. This may immediately suggest a certain type of design. A cushion must look good when the cushion is seen from any angle, so this limits the design to start with.

Choose your fabric—its colour, texture, washability, hard-wearing qualities and so on—bearing its purpose in mind. Then choose the type of thread, trying out different ones and different numbers of strands to see what looks best on the fabric. At the same time you will be trying out stitches as well and be forming an idea of which ones you would like to use. The next thing is to decide how much of the fabric you are going to embroider, and where the design is to be placed. It is important to consider the general effect of the colours at this stage too, whether it is going to have more light shades than dark, as this will affect the positioning of the design.

It is probably a good idea to cut a piece of paper into the size of the finished article, then cut out the general shape of the design you are considering so you can move it around on the paper. One particular pitfall is the proportion. Never have half the fabric embroidered and half left blank and never use equal quantities of two colours of thread, as this never works. You may find your cut shape is the wrong size in any position and needs to be larger or smaller. Experiment until you think you have got the balance exactly right. Leave the shape on the paper while you consider the colours.

Care is needed in the choice of a colour scheme, which is much easier to live with if it is limited to several shades of one colour and a little contrasting colour than if you use a great variety of colours. Experience will show when extra colour can be allowed. Do not have colours all the same tone either. It is not necessary to stick to real-life colours and often designs work much better when you do not.

The shape of the flower, or whatever the motif is, is still there whichever colour has been used. Remember here to take into account where the embroidery is going to be. If you plan a picture to hang in the bedroom, then the colour scheme of the bedroom must be considered; a traycloth will not look good if its colours clash with the colours of your tea cups. Colours do move in and out of fashion, so if you want to work a very modern piece, you will have to bear this in mind. If you look through magazines and look at modern fabrics you should get an idea, if you are in doubt.

The next stage is to decide on the actual design—flowers, geometric shapes, or whatever you prefer. Make sure the subject is suitable for the use the article will be put to—you probably would not want snakes on a pillow-case for instance. The shapes must be right for the type of work as well. Again, you can cut shapes in paper and move them about. Once you have chosen the shapes, you can trace the design and then transfer it to the fabric (see page 50). If it is to be a piece of counted-thread work you will have to work the threads out on your tracing.

The final stage, before actually embroidering, is to choose the proportions of the colours to be used and the stitches, though of course variations can be made as you go along. Remember that couching with a thick white thread on a dark fabric is going to add much more light to the design than a line of back stitches, which will add very little. Do not use a free-style stitch when all the others are geometric. Remember that tiny stitching is wasted on a large bold design and big loose stitches are useless for household linen which is to be washed frequently.

Design does not always come easily, but the actual process of drawing need not be a stumbling block. Several kinds of embroidery develop their patterns directly from the stitches themselves, needing no preliminary sketches; drawn-thread and drawn-fabric work are good examples. In surface stitchery many of the most beautiful peasant designs are composed of simple shapes repeated over and over again in different colours, tones and stitches.

If you cannot draw with a pencil, you may be able to cut good pattern shapes out of paper with a pair of scissors or perhaps you can paint well. Ideas for designs may come in all sorts of ways. Basic shapes, like the circle, square, triangle and so on, have been used since olden days in architecture, textiles, mosiacs, frescoes and even traditional knitting patterns.

Nature gives many ideas: as well as visits to zoos and gardens, there are birds, wild flowers, fields, streams, trees and many other things which you can look at for ideas. It is always good to look at other people's work, so when you get the chance to visit a museum or go to an exhibition you should always take the opportunity to study historic examples of needlework.

Special points for beginners

Choose very even-weave fabric whether you are doing counted-thread work or free-style. It will help you to work even stitches, and to get any lines straight. It is probably easiest to work with twisted cotton of one thickness to start with. You can use the old-fashioned method for getting the correct length of thread— this is the same as the distance from your finger to your elbow. Remember, you must practise your stitches before you start.

One of the easiest starting-off designs for a beginner is a band across an edge, say, of a tray cloth. If you do a border all the way round you will have to consider how the stitches are to be worked at each corner, so a band is much easier. Do not forget to allow for the hem when deciding where the band is to go. Plan rows of stitches across the band and decide which stitch you want to work in the middle first. You may have decided on some definite stitches when you practised beforehand. Embroider this middle row on to the material first. It is a good idea to work in one colour, perhaps in two different thicknesses, or two shades of one colour, as this allows the stitches to form the pattern not the colour.

After you have worked a band, you will want to move on, perhaps to geometric patterns and counted-thread work, perhaps to a free-style pattern. Counted-thread designs need to be worked out mathematically before you start; free-style designs need to be transferred carefully from paper to fabric so you know exactly where your stitches are to go. Stitches can be grouped in straight, waved or zig-zag lines, or in circles, triangles or other shapes. Simple outline stitches are running, back, whipped back (which makes a more definite line) and couching (which is even more defined). Fancy outline stitches include herringbone and feather.

If you are a beginner there is a definite advantage in joining a class for embroidery. Not only do you get the expert advice of the teacher, but seeing different techniques, fabrics and colours being used gives you ideas for new work.

When things go wrong

The worst thing is knowing that your design hasn't quite worked and not knowing why. You must learn to look at your work with a critical eye, as you are working the embroidery as well as afterwards. Do not fall into the trap of leaving a large or important area of the design blank in the hope that you will have some great inspiration for it. You get so used to seeing the space empty, it becomes more and more impossible to find a way of filling it. Do not continue steadfastly embroidering with your planned colours and stitches when you know in your heart of hearts they are not turning out quite right. A slight alteration could make all the difference: a touch of extra colour here, or more light shades on one side of the design, or a thicker outline there. Perhaps you should put the embroidery away for a few days and return to it with a fresh eye.

After the embroidery is finished you may still be able to make adjustments, if you think something is wrong, without unpicking. If it looks in the wrong position, perhaps you can alter the hem, making it smaller or larger to make the design nearer or farther away from the edge. Perhaps you can add a line of stitching or fringe the hem. Would a piped edging or tassels help a cushion, or an additional outline, possibly in running stitch, help a certain part of the design? If no simple alteration is sufficient then you will have to unpick something, but think very hard before restitching as you don't want to make another mistake.

If the embroidery is disastrously wrong, ask yourself whether the design was wrong to start with. Perhaps the idea was too grand for the method of working, or unsuitable for the item you were making. Was the design three-dimensional instead of flat? Were the wrong stitches used, or were they too big or too small or just not good enough because you didn't practise enough? Should you have used a frame when you did not?

If you can find out why you have gone wrong then you will be able to avoid the same snags next time and your designing will improve.

Green silk shoes embroidered with silver thread.

Counted-thread work

Surviving examples of medieval German whitework on church linen show that satin stitch was being worked over counted threads at that time. Counted-thread patterns in black silk on linen originated on the continent. They reached England in the time of Henry VIII, but at first their use was limited to borders of double running at neck and wrist on men's shirts and women's shifts. Gradually designs became more and more elaborate with scrolling stems supporting leaves, flowers or fruit. Many small, elaborate geometric patterns were developed, all strongly outlined, and these decorated coifs, tunics, dresses and cushions. An interest in blackwork has revived today but the strict counted-thread discipline of earlier times is not now applied so rigidly. Outlines are not considered absolutely essential; shapes can be defined by changes in tone made by dense and open patterns.

The beginner is often daunted by the thought of counting the threads of a fabric for each stitch, but this should not be so. It is not necessary to have a very fine fabric; even-weave linen threads can easily be counted. There is no need to transfer the design on to the fabric as counted-thread work can be worked from a chart. And it's much easier to work even stitches with counted-thread work than it is with free-style embroidery.

Many of the stitches given in the chapter beginning on page 55 can be used with counted-thread work, for instance back, whipped back, double running, cross, long-armed cross, double knot and satin stitches. Some special counted-thread stitches and more variations of cross stitch are given here.

Cushion cover worked in four-sided stitch and stars of satin stitches on an evenweave fabric.

A modern interpretation of Elizabethan blackwork—the fish design is worked in brown threads instead of traditional black. A sheet of aluminium kitchen foil under the fabric gives an attractive sparkle to the finished piece.

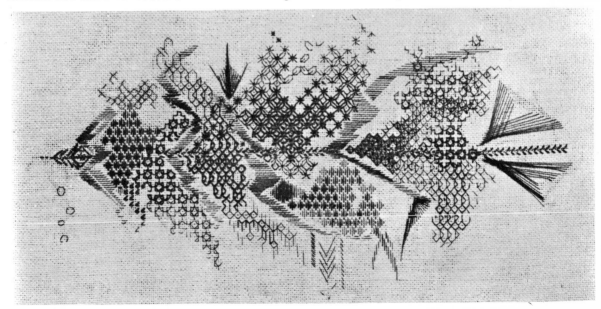

DOUBLE CROSS STITCH

Work a single cross stitch over 4 threads in normal way. Bring needle out in centre of bottom of cross. Insert needle at centre of top of cross then bring out again at centre of left side of cross. Insert at centre of right of cross. Finish off or bring needle out ready for next cross stitch.

DIAGONAL RAISED BAND

 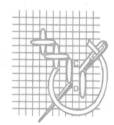

Work diagonally from lower right to top left corner. Bring needle out at lower right corner. Make a vertical stitch up over 4 threads, then bring out again 2 threads down and 2 threads to the left. Continue in this way to top of row and bring needle out as if to begin another stitch. Work a horizontal stitch over 4 threads, then bring needle out again 2 threads down and 2 threads to the left. Repeat to end of row.

MONTENEGRIN CROSS STITCH

Work from left to right. Bring needle out at bottom of cross at left. Insert needle 8 threads to right and 4 threads up, then bring out 4 threads to right of starting point. Insert again 4 threads up from starting point and bring out in same place as last time. Insert 4 threads up and bring out again at same place as last time. Continue along row.

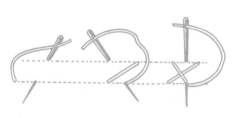 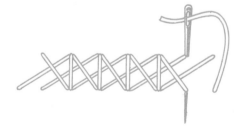

MOSAIC FILLING

Work 4 blocks of 4 satin stitches (see page 65) over 3 threads each to form a square as shown in diagram. Now bring thread through at bottom right corner of inner square. Work a four-sided stitch (see page 92) in inner square, bringing thread out again at starting point. Work a cross stitch in centre.

RICE STITCH

This is usually worked in a thick thread for the large cross stitch and a fine thread for the small straight stitch. Work a row of cross stitch (see page 59) over 4 threads each way. With thinner thread work diagonal stitches over 2 threads each over the corners of each cross stitch as shown in diagram.

TWO-SIDED CROSS STITCH

This stitch makes a cross on both sides of the work. Four journeys in each row are necessary.

Work first row from right to left, starting at bottom right corner of first cross. Insert needle 4 threads up and 4 threads to the left and bring out again 8 threads from starting point to the left. Continue along row so both sides have one diagonal stroke worked. On second row work in same way but from left to right. At end of second row make a half cross stitch back to centre of cross, then another up to top right corner, then work along row as before. Work fourth row as before, from left to right, to complete all crosses on both sides.

CROSS-STITCH DESIGNS

Cross stitch was used during the Coptic period in Egypt— the first few centuries of the Christian era—and has been used throughout Europe, North Africa and the Middle East.

It is seen at its best on peasant costume of Slavonic countries. Some of the most beautiful peasant embroideries in the world have been worked in cross stitch, often only in one colour. Many are so strongly constructed they would not lose their impact if they were worked only in black on white. The secret of much of their success lies in the arrangement of stitches in blocks, so shaped that they in turn make shapes of the background spaces, so two patterns result, dark on light, and light on dark.

The material used for cross-stitch designs should be of even-weave so the threads can be counted. No transfer will ever be as successful as counting threads. Linen, voile, hessian and hopsack are all good as well as some modern furnishing fabrics. Printed check material can be used, working the crosses in the squares instead of counting the threads.

Almost any thread can be used, provided it looks good on the material; a coarse fabric usually needs a coarse thread. Bright colours are often used. The method of working ordinary cross stitch, both individually and in rows, is given on page 59 The crosses may be worked over as many threads as liked.

DOUBLE RUNNING EMBROIDERY

Double running or Holbein stitch is one of the easiest to work (see page 65). In the 17th century very elaborate designs were worked in double running, but the stitch was used earlier than this. A fragment of a robe worked in ancient Egypt is decorated with narrow borders of double running, worked in dark grey silk thread. It has been used much in Islamic embroideries, and, combined with cross stitch, is used in Assisi work.

Graph paper is helpful in working out a double running design. The stitches must stay the same length throughout the work, and can be horizontal, vertical, or diagonal. The result

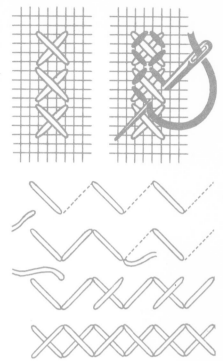

should look exactly the same from both sides of the work. Even-weave fabric should be used, the warp and weft threads being of the same thickness. Working thread should.be chosen so that it is the same thickness as well. A white or natural-coloured linen worked with black or dark-coloured thread looks very attractive, but any strong colour such as red, green, blue or yellow can be used. Two colours may be mixed if liked. Stranded cotton, *coton à broder* and pearl cotton are often chosen. A tapestry needle can be used in order not to split the threads of the fabric.

Before beginning to stitch it is wise to work out the route your needle is going to take, as side shoots must be worked as you go along, though some may be worked on the first journey and some on the second. As work should look the same on both sides, thread must never cut across a space or cut a corner on the back. To begin and finish thread, run end of thread on right side through weave of fabric along stitch line where it will be covered by the double running. On the second journey, the needle should be inserted into the same hole as on the first, but just above the thread of the stitch made on the first journey. It should be brought out just below stitch made on first journey. Making sure you work every stitch in the same way like this will gives the work a neater finish.

ASSISI WORK

Assisi work takes its name from the modern embroideries made in Assisi, Italy. Earliest examples are 16th century, but were not known by this name then. Traditional designs are composed of stylised animals, birds and grotesques, similar to those found in Renaissance ornament. In early works the design always had a dark outline and the background was usually red, but occasionally green and brown have been used. The essential characteristic of Assisi work is that the design is left uncovered or void, the background being completely worked in cross stitch, or long-armed cross stitch.

Double running (Holbein) stitches outline the design. The technique demands a formal design, but not necessarily the Renaissance style now so out of keeping with our time. Experiments have been made successfully working fine flannel, the threads of which are even and easily counted, with crewel wool, with Lurex thread darned in lines between borders, supported by double running stitch in *coton à broder*. The normal use of Assisi work is for table linen, cloths, cushions, banners, hangings and bags, but this new type of work offers fresh opportunities for design.

Squared paper is helpful for planning a design. Each line must follow the outline of a square, either vertically or horizontally. No diagonal lines can be used as this would split a square in two and you would not be able to work a cross stitch in it. Many cross-stitch patterns can be adapted by reversing the position of stitch and background. It should be remembered that Assisi work is essentially design in mass, not line. The borders of the work are improved by placing lines of four-sided stitch (see page 92) or double-running stitch on either side of the Assisi borders.

White or natural-coloured linen is the usual choice for fabric. Only two different colours of thread should be used: a dark shade such as black, brown, green or red for outlining the design in double running, and a light contrasting shade for the background cross stitches. Double running stitches in black and cross stitches in blue or rust are often used.

The design is far more important than the colours. *Coton à broder*, stranded cotton and pearl cotton are suitable threads for work on linen. Work the outline in double running first, and do not carry the thread over a space or cut a corner on the back. If the double running has been worked over 3 threads then each cross will be worked in a 3-thread square. The border should be worked last, and it is usual for the work to have a tightly rolled hem rather than a folded one.

ROUMANIAN EMBROIDERY

This is another combination of cross stitch and double running. It differs from Assisi work in that the motifs are worked in cross stitch and the background is left uncovered. Small offshoots in double running are attached to the cross-stitch motifs, giving a delicate touch to them. The same rules apply as for Assisi work. Roumanian work can be done in one colour or many different colours. If only one colour is used, then the double running offshoots can be worked at the same time as the cross stitch. If a gay colour is being used for the cross stitch, the double running looks good if worked in black thread.

White net dress, embroidered with gold thread. Underdress is in white satin, 1820—5.

Cutwork

Cutwork derives from Italian 16th-century *point coupé*. Venetian laces were very famous and in demand all over Europe. Because of high taxes on the lace, Cardinal Richelieu sent for Italian lacemakers to work in France and they set up schools and workshops. Richelieu work, which is slightly more complicated than simple cutwork, was named after the Cardinal.

The work was extremely popular in the 17th century, and much used up to the beginning of this century, when it rather fell out of favour. Nowadays it is used mainly to decorate table linen. Comparatively little is done except in Italy which produces very fine needlework in professional workshops.

Basically cutwork consists of a design outlined in buttonhole stitch with the background cut away. Both simple cutwork and Richelieu work are normally embroidered on firm linen which does not fray easily, and look best when the fabric is white or natural-coloured. It is difficult to cut the edge of a soft material, but if you do use one, back the design with organdie before working and cut it away afterwards. The thread should be the same colour as the linen because background spaces made when the fabric is cut away help to form the design; this is confused by the introduction of other colours.

Cutwork picture of lambs and blossom.

SIMPLE CUTWORK

First of all the design must be considered very carefully. It must be compact, with all parts linked to each other, or to the main fabric so that when the background is cut away the material does not fall to pieces, or leave part of the design hanging loose. The total area of background spaces should be less than the area of the main surface (the fabric without cutwork).

Transfer the design to the fabric by the prick and pounce method (see page 51); purchased transfers are available for cutwork too and should be transferred in the usual way. Work 2 rows of running stitch just inside the outline to strengthen the edge. You can work more rows of running stitch if you want to pad the outline, though as the buttonhole stitch is worked very close together, the result will be fairly well embossed anyway. Now work buttonhole stitch round the outline of the design, including those parts which will not be cut round, with the heading of the buttonhole stitch against the edge which will be cut.

The width of the buttonhole stitch may vary if this adds to the design; otherwise make sure your stitches are of even length and close together to prevent any fraying later on. Cutting away the fabric is the last operation, to be worked when all the buttonholing is complete. Use very sharp-pointed scissors, work on right side and cut close to buttonhole stitches, but being careful not to cut into them. If you do not cut close to the stitching, the fabric will fray out. Press the work carefully face downwards on a soft pad.

RICHELIEU WORK

This was known as Renaissance work in the 19th century. In Richelieu work, the design may contain free motifs which are held to the main fabric by bars. These bars strengthen the work, and also add variety to the design. Richelieu work looks much more decorative than simple cutwork.

Start working as for simple cutwork. Work the first row of running stitch close to outline, and when you meet a bar work as follows.

Carry thread over to opposite motif which is to be held by same bar, and take a small stitch within the area that will be covered by buttonholing. Carry thread across to first side again

A border of cutwork worked in Ireland, late 19th century.

and take a small stitch there. Take thread back to second side and take a final short stitch. You now have 3 threads joining motifs. Work buttonhole stitch over the 3 threads, without needle entering fabric, so you end up on first side again. You can now continue with the running-stitch outline until you meet the next bar. After working the first round of running stitch, continue as for simple cutwork, working a second round, then the button-holing. When cutting the background away, cut all fabric underneath bars.

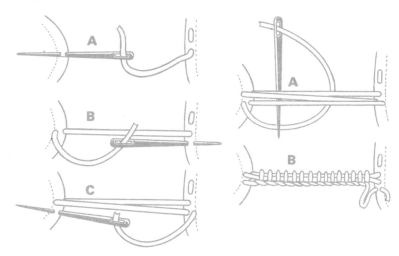

The bars must be worked evenly and kept firm so that they do not sag when the material underneath is cut away. They may also be worked in cording if this is preferred. The 3 threads are taken across in the usual way, but instead of working button-hole stitch, work round them as for oversewing—again without needle entering fabric. The cording must be worked very close together.

A buttonhole bar can be decorated with a picot, which makes the work even more rich and lacy. Picots can appear fussy, so don't overdo them.

Work buttonhole stitch to halfway along bar. Now pass the thread over the bar without making the knot of the buttonhole stitch, leaving a loop below. Hold the loop with a pin. Take the needle under the 3 threads and over the working thread from left to right as shown in the diagram. Remove pin. Continue with buttonhole stitching along bar.

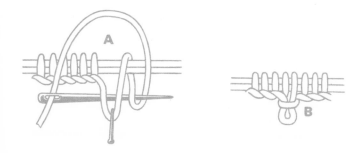

Drawn-fabric and drawn-thread work

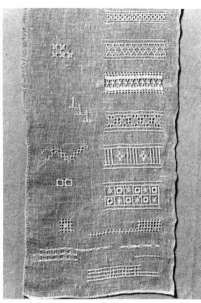

Drawn (or pulled) fabric sampler.

In drawn-fabric work special stitches are worked over fabric and pulled tightly to draw threads of fabric together, so producing an openwork pattern. In drawn-thread work the warp or weft threads are withdrawn from the fabric, and remaining threads gathered together.

DRAWN-FABRIC WORK

Drawn-fabric work is of peasant origin and believed to have spread to various European countries from the Greek islands in the 17th and 18th centuries. It is essentially a technique for loosely woven material: muslin, linen, fine woollens or any fabric which allows its threads to be parted easily. On a sheer fabric it is sometimes known as embroidered lace and stitches may be referred to as lace fillings. Stitches are worked by counting the threads of the fabric and pulling the needle tightly so a space forms between the threads of the fabric. A fragile appearance results, but the fabric remains strong and hard-wearing.

Provided the scale of stitch is in keeping with the area to be covered, any simple shape may be filled; alternatively the

Tea cosy in Hardanger work.

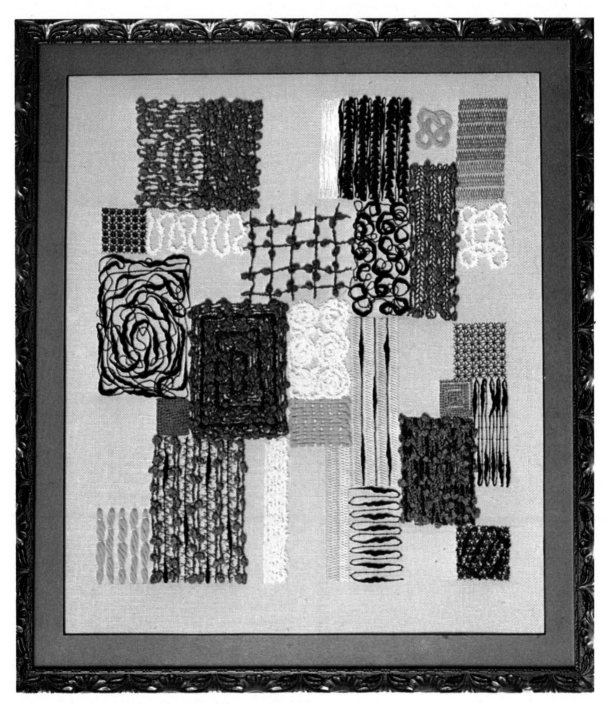

Couching sampler, using various weaving yarns.

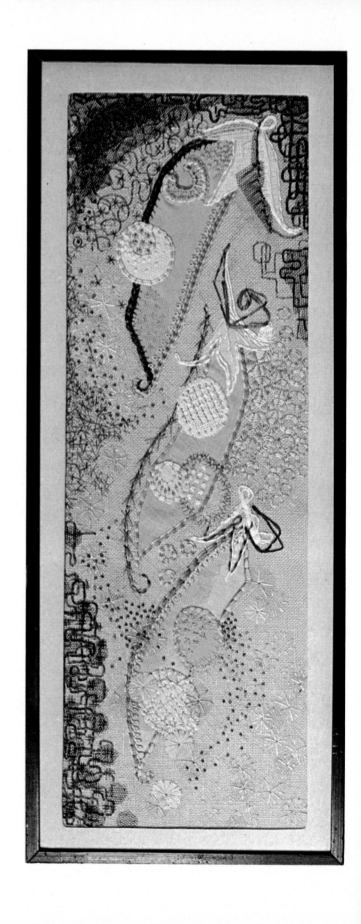

'Pea Pods', a modern design in surface stitchery.

background may be covered and the design left free. A frame should be used and if this is a Swiss ring a piece of soft material put between hoops and fabric. Originally stitches were worked on white or natural-coloured linen with matching thread. This still looks very attractive, but coloured fabrics with matching or contrasting threads are also used. A tapestry needle will part the threads without splitting them.

DRAWN-FABRIC STITCHES
Algerian eye or star eyelet

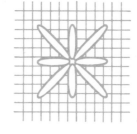

This consists of 8 stitches worked from the same centre. It is usually worked in diagonal rows and, as it is a very open stitch, care must be taken when transferring from one star to the next. Start with top right diagonal stitch, work to centre then bring needle out again at top to work vertical stitch to centre. Continue round star in this way.

Back stitch

This is worked in the same way as given on page 55, but when it is pulled tightly the thread between the stitches becomes obvious and so should be considered as part of the design.

Double back stitch

This too is worked in the same way as instructed on page 55, but is best worked on the wrong side by using closed herringbone stitch. When the stitches are pulled tightly a raised effect is made.

Chessboard filling stitch

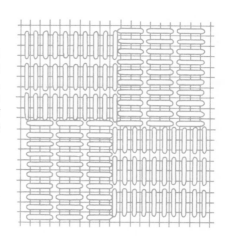

This consists of rectangular blocks of satin stitch (see page 65) worked vertically and horizontally as shown in diagram. Each satin stitch is worked over 3 threads of fabric and pulled tightly, and each block is composed of 3 rows of 10 stitches. A thin thread works better for this filling than a thick one and a finer needle than a tapestry one is helpful to darn ends of thread into lines of stitchery.

Cobbler filling stitch

Work horizontal rows first. Start at bottom right corner and make a stitch vertically over 4 threads; bring needle out again 4 threads to left of starting point. Make another vertical stitch over 4 threads then bring needle out 2 threads to left on bottom line. Continue in this way working vertical stitches alternately after 4 threads and 2 threads to end of row. Leave 2 threads before starting second row which is worked in exactly same way as first, but left to right. Continue until all horizontal rows are worked, then turn fabric round at right angles to work vertical rows in exactly same way.

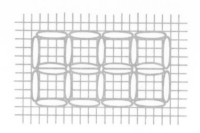

Four-sided stitch

This stitch can be used as a border or filling. Work from right to left. Bring needle through at bottom right corner of first stitch. Insert needle 4 threads up and bring out again 4 threads to left of starting point. Insert needle at starting point and bring out 4 threads up and 4 threads to left. Insert 4 threads to right, bring out 4 threads to left of starting point. For a single stitch, work final side of square. For a row, continue as before. Pull all stitches firmly.

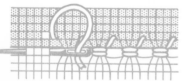

Honeycomb filling stitch

Work from top to bottom. Start at top left corner and bring thread through. Make a horizontal stitch across 4 threads to the right, then bring out 4 threads down. Insert 4 threads up and bring out again 4 threads down. Make a horizontal stitch to left across 4 threads, then bring needle up 4 threads down. Take needle 4 threads up then bring out 4 threads down. Continue in this way to bottom of row, but do not work last stitch of sequence. Turn fabric round and work in same way as first row for second row. Continue. All stitches should be pulled tightly.

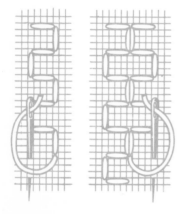

Mosaic filling stitch

This is worked in the same way as described on page 80, except that stitches are pulled tightly.

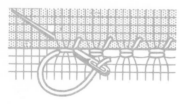

Pin stitch

This is used along a hem edge.
Work from right to left. Bring thread through folded hem edge 2 threads in then make a vertical stitch over the 2 threads into main fabric. Bring needle out 4 threads to left, insert back at previous point on main fabric, then bring out again through folded hem 4 threads to left and 2 threads down.

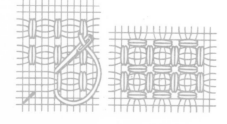

Punch stitch

Work horizontal rows first. Work from right to left. Make 2 vertical stitches over 4 threads in the same place, then bring needle out 4 stitches to left for next 2 stitches. Continue along row in this way, and then work all other horizontal rows in same way, turning fabric round for each. Turn fabric at right angles, and work vertical rows in same way as horizontal.

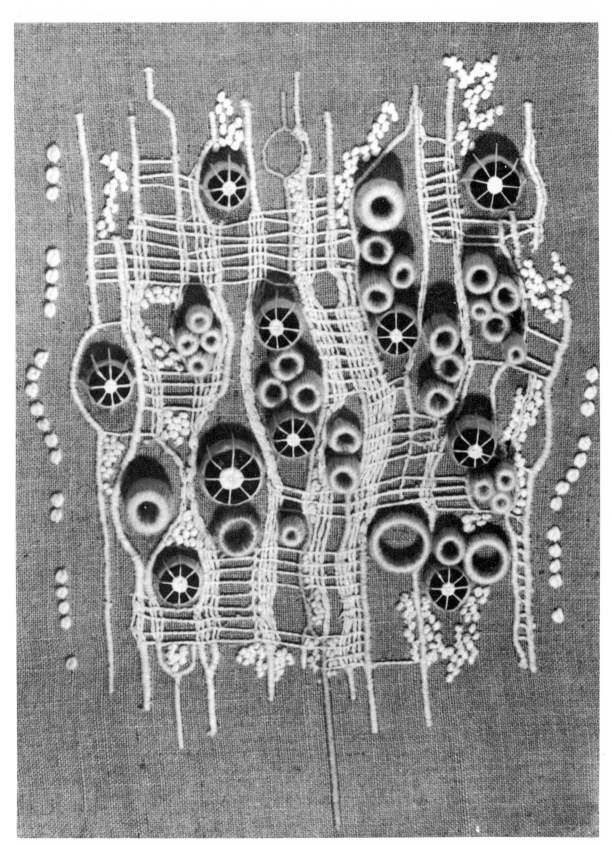

'Oodles', an embroidered panel worked by a schoolgirl.

Ringed back stitch

Work from right to left. Bring needle through fabric and insert 3 threads down. Bring out 6 threads up and 3 threads to left and insert at starting point. Bring needle out 3 threads up and 6 threads to left and insert 3 threads back. Continue making back stitches like this, following outline on diagram. When row is complete, turn fabric round and work back in same way as before. All connecting stitches are worked into same holes.

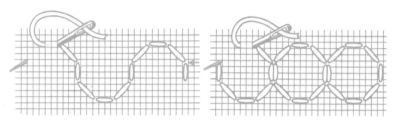

Three-sided stitch

Work from right to left. Start 4 threads in from end of stitch line and work two horizontal stitches from this point to end of line. Bring needle through at starting point and make two stitches to point 4 threads up and 2 threads to right. Bring needle through 4 threads to left of point and work 2 stitches back to point, bring needle through again 4 threads to left. Make 2 stitches to starting point then bring needle through 4 threads to left ready to start next stitch. Continue in this way.

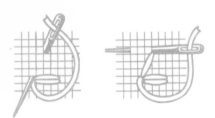

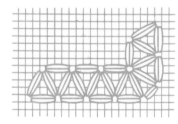

Wave stitch filling

Work from right to left. Bring needle up 2 threads in from end. Make first stitch 2 threads to the right and 4 threads up then bring needle out again 4 threads to left. Insert needle at starting point and bring out 4 threads to the left. Continue in this way to end of row. To work next row turn fabric round then work in same way as before.

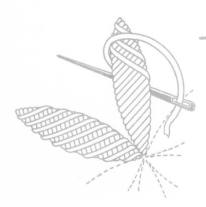
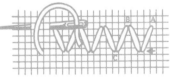
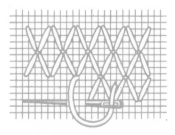

Whipped satin stitch

Work satin stitch as described on page 65, except that each stitch is pulled tight. Work whipping stitches at right angles as shown in diagram.

DRAWN-THREAD WORK

In drawn-thread work a number of either the warp or the weft threads are cut and drawn out of the material, leaving the remaining threads to be protected and decorated in one of several different ways. Drawn-thread work is seen in the embroideries of many European countries, particularly Norway, Hungary and Sicily, and in parts of Asia. Generally the thread used matches the background fabric, white or natural coloured being the most common. However Hungarian and Roumanian national costumes include blouses beautifully decorated in drawn-thread hem stitch in bright colours—turquoise, red, orange and yellow. Drawn-thread work is most used today for household linen and lingerie and handkerchiefs.

Cotton and linen are the fabrics most often chosn for this type of work, though other fabrics, such as canvas or organdie, can be used. The warp and the weft threads should be as near the same thickness as possible.

Hem stitch

Drawn-thread work is often used to make a decorative hem, and the first step is to withdraw the threads. Decide on the length of the hem then withdraw the first thread two threads above this. To do this pull out the thread near the edge of the material then take it firmly and pull right out from across the whole width of the material. The number of threads you withdraw will depend upon the fabric and the pattern you intend to work. A fine fabric needs only a few threads taken out, a heavier fabric needs more.

Danish linen drawn-thread sampler, 18th century.

Drawn-thread mat, with mitred corners.

When threads are taken out on all four sides of a piece of cloth, a little more care is needed. First mark off the depth of the hem round each corner. The threads to be withdrawn must be cut $\frac{1}{2}$ in. in from the hem and only the centre threads taken out. These $\frac{1}{2}$-in. ends are then folded back so they will lie in the hem. A square hole is left at each corner, the corner must be mitred before hem stitch is worked. The stitching may be worked with the withdrawn threads, or a thread of similar weight to threads of fabric. It should be strong and smooth, but not too heavy. Stranded cotton, pearl cotton or *coton à broder* would be suitable for linen.

Simple hem stitch

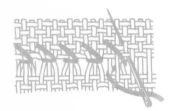

Draw out 2 or 3 threads from the fabric then turn up the hem to 1 thread from first withdrawn thread (with corners mitred if work is going round four sides). Work on wrong side from left to right, with hem at top. Fasten thread at left then pass thread from right to left under 3 or 4 of the border threads, bring needle out and pass it from below upwards under 1 or 2 threads of turning at right of group of threads. When a corner is reached, work buttonhole stitches close together over both edges of hem.

Ladder hem stitch

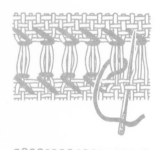

This is worked in exactly the same way as simple hem stitch, but both edges of the drawn-thread border are worked.

Zig-zag hem stitch

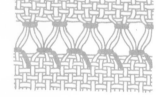

Begin by working simple hem stitch along one edge, but be sure to pick up an even number of border threads each line. Then work the other edge, taking half the threads from one group and half from the next group together, as shown in the diagram. The row will start and finish with half a group.

Double hem stitch or Italian hem stitch

Withdraw threads from the fabric in the usual way, then miss the same number of threads and withdraw another band of the same number of threads above. Working from right to left on the right side, bring thread out 4 border threads to the left on the top band. Pass the needle over and then behind the 4 threads; bring it out again at starting point. Now take thread over fabric between bands and behind next 4 threads on lower band. Take needle over 4 threads and insert then bring out again on top band 4 threads across to the left. Continue along row. The two other edges of the drawn-thread borders can be worked with simple hem stitch.

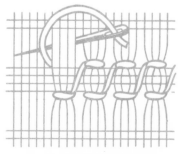
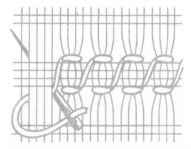

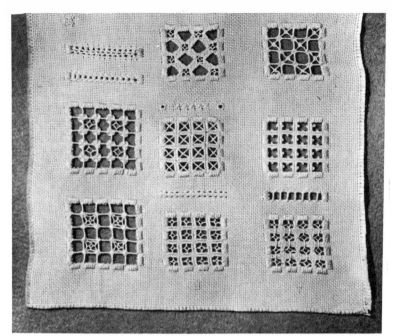

TYING THE THREADS

A simple, narrow drawn-thread border needs no further decoration but a wider one will need the threads worked by crossing the groups, knotting them or by working decorative motifs.

Crossing groups of threads or interlaced hemstitch

First work ladder hemstitch along the edges of the border. The interlacing can be worked with the same thread or a slightly thicker one. Secure along thread at right-hand edge of border. Take needle across two groups of threads then take it back under the first group and over the second. Pull needle through then bring it back up again ready to work over next 2 groups.

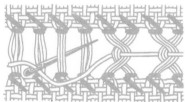
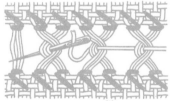

Threads may also be crossed, working in a similar way, by taking half of the first group and crossing it with half of the next group (diagram A), by crossing 2 whole groups with 4 half-groups (diagram B), and by crossing two pairs of groups at a time (diagram C).

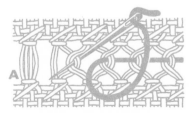
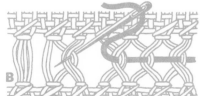

Drawn-thread fillings.

Knotting groups of threads

Groups of threads can be knotted singly, or 2, 3 or more at a time, and can be worked in 1 row or several parallel rows. The thread used can be visible or hidden in the threads. Diagram A shows 3 groups of threads being knotted together with the thread visible. Attach thread to right edge of border (ladder hemstitch having been worked along edges of border). Take thread over 3 groups and hold as for chain stitch. The needle is then passed under the groups from right to left and up over working thread. Pull needle through and a knot forms over the groups.

Diagram B shows groups knotted in pairs close to one edge of border, then knotted again close to other edge taking half of first knotted group with half of second knotted group. Diagram C shows groups of 3 knotted without thread being seen. Carry thread along edge of border until third group is reached. Wind thread round this group to middle then work knot in usual way over the 3 groups. Wind thread round group again back to edge of border.

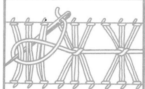

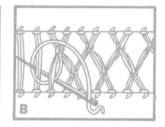

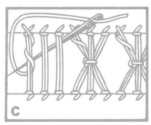

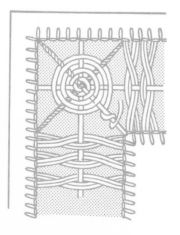

CORNERS

When 6 threads or more have been removed, the empty corner space will need to be decorated, with a wheel or web. The corner has already had buttonhole stitch worked round it when the hem stitch was worked and if groups of threads have been crossed or knotted there will also be two threads going across, making 4 spokes of the wheel. Eight spokes must be made in all. Fasten the thread to one corner and take it diagonally across to other corner. Now twist thread back to centre, then out to another corner, twist back to centre, carry out to fourth corner, twist back to centre. Where the threads cross in the centre a wheel is worked by winding the thread round the centre, over and under alternate spokes. Finish by twisting thread out to first corner.

Finishing touches

Hems finished with drawn-thread work have already been described in the chapter beginning on page 88. There are various other ways of finishing off edges, which are described in this chapter. Threads should be chosen according to your fabric, probably the same type as has been used in main embroidery.

DECORATIVE EDGING STITCHES

Two of the most simple edging stitches are overcast stitch and buttonhole stitch. These can be worked over a raw edge, when they should be worked very close together, or over a finished edge. When a hem has been turned up, coral stitch (see page 58) can be worked along the fold; this both holds the hem in place and gives an attractive finish. Blanket stitch is another which can be worked along a finished edge, and may be used with either the tops of the vertical stitches or the knotted end of stitches along the edge.

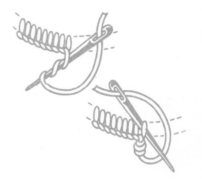

Scalloped buttonhole edge

Scallops are best made with a template cut out of thick paper or cardboard the size you have decided upon. Lay the template on the fabric along the edge and draw round it with a hard pencil. Move template round fabric until scallops have been drawn all round. Now move the template up a little and draw an inner line all round—this will give you a guide to the length of your stitches when you are sewing. A line of running stitches may be worked between the two lines if padding is required on wide scallops. Now work buttonhole stitches very close together all round scallop edge.

Buttonhole stitch with picots

Work as for ordinary buttonhole stitch round edge until required position for picot is reached. Hold the thread down with the left thumb and twist the needle 3 times round the thread. Still holding thread firmly, pull working thread until twisted threads are close to stitching, then work a buttonhole stitch into upright part of last buttonhole stitch, as shown in diagram.

Knot stitch edging

This is sometimes called Antwerp edging. Bring thread through from back of fabric, and work a buttonhole stitch loosely. Pass needle behind loop of stitch and over working thread as shown in diagram. It can be spaced out to make a lacy edging or worked close together. More rows can be made, working over loops of previous row.

Two fringed shawls from the Amager district of Denmark, 19th century. The shawls are in silk embroidered with coloured silks in satin, long and short, split and chain stitches.

CROCHET EDGINGS
Loop picot edge
The edge may first be sewn with overcasting stitches or not, as preferred. A suitable thread is pearl cotton or crochet cotton; work with a small hook.
    *Work 1 double crochet into edge of hem, 5 chain, 1 treble into first chain; repeat from * right round edge.

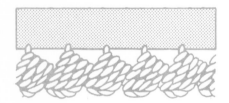

Treble picot edge
The same threads as for the loop picot may be used.
    *Work 1 treble into edge, 3 chain, working sideways into treble below, work 3 treble; repeat from * right round edge.

FRINGING
Raw edges of a piece of work may be fringed, with the fabric protected by a line of hem stitch or four-sided stitch.

Hem stitch (see page 95)
Draw out 1 or 2 threads $\frac{3}{4}$ to 1in. from the edge. On this line work hem stitch from wrong side, binding threads in groups of 3 or 4 and taking up 2 threads of main fabric. When the hem stitch is completed, pull away all the outer threads to make the fringe.

Four-sided stitch (see page 92)
Draw out 1 or 2 threads $\frac{3}{4}$ to 1in. from the edge. On this line work four-sided stitch tightly on right side of material about $\frac{3}{4}$ to 1in. from the edge. Fringe outer edge by pulling out all the outer threads.

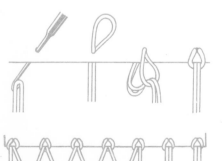

Decorating the fringe
Additional threads, perhaps in another colour, can be added to the fringe in the following way. Cut thread into pieces twice as long as you require for fringe. Taking about 6 lengths at a time knot into lower edge: fold lengths in half, then use a crochet hook to draw the looped ends through the edge of the fabric. Draw ends through loops and pull tight.
Knotting. The fringe may be knotted in 2 rows. In the first row knot two adjacent groups of threads together all round edge. For the second row, knot half of first group with half of second group and continue round in this way. A half group is left at beginning of work to be knotted with a half group which will be left over at end.

TASSELS

Tassels can be added to a fringed edge, or sewn on to a plain edge, or attached to a cord which is sewn on to the edge.

To make a tassel

Wind thread round a piece of card the length of tassel required until fairly thick. With a tapestry needle take a thread under loops at one end of card and draw together and knot, leaving ends of thread to sew with. Cut through loops along bottom then wind a thread round tassel just below top and fasten. Trim ends. If looped ends are required, work in the same way but slide card out without cutting through loops at bottom.

To make a twisted cord

Take several lengths of thread at least 4 times the length required for finished cord. Tie the ends and fold in half. Attach looped end to some fixed point—a nail in the wall or a door knob. Take ends and twist round and round in the same direction until tight. Now put two ends together and let the rest twist itself together.

POMPONS

Pompons are often used to decorate furnishings.

Cut 2 cirlces of card the diameter of required pompon. Cut a hole in the middle of each, this hole having a diameter $\frac{1}{4}$ the size of circle. Put the 2 circles together and wind thread over card and through centre hole, working round card until centre hole is full. Cut through strands round outside edge with scissors between pieces of card. Wind a single strand of thread very tightly between cards and fasten securely. Pull cards off and fluff out pompons. Trim ends if necessary.

WASHING EMBROIDERIES

Most modern threads are colour-fast, and as long as your fabric is washable embroideries can be washed quite safely. Use lukewarm water and soap flakes, and squeeze embroidery gently in the water; do not rub or twist. Rinse well in lukewarm water.

Press embroidery on wrong side while still damp, being careful to check that iron is not too hot. A damp cloth may be placed between embroidery and iron, in which case the embroidery may be a little drier. Have a thick pad of material on ironing board so embroidery is not flattened.

MOUNTING AND FRAMING

If you want your embroidery framed, it is best to have it done professionally. It is possible to have your work professionally stitched and mounted too, if you wish.

It is fairly easy to mount your embroidery on cardboard or hardboard. Place embroidery centrally over the board, and fold surplus fabric to the back. Secure embroidery at top with drawing pins into edge of board, then pull firmly over lower edge so embroidery is quite taut. Secure by lacing edges together. Do the same with the sides of the embroidery: the diagram shows the finished result. Remove drawing pins. If wished, a sheet of paper or thin card may be glued lightly in place over back of work to hide the lacing.

Machine embroidery

In recent years machine embroidery has been recognised as an important branch of the craft of embroidery. Some machine embroidery can be worked with any type of sewing machine; free embroidery needs both hands and so must be worked with a treadle machine or an electric one. You don't need to be experienced either in hand embroideries or in dressmaking to be successful at machine embroidery. It takes practice to operate the machine properly, but then hand stitches need practising too before they are mastered and worked evenly.

Machine embroidery does not set out to imitate hand embroidery; sometimes it is combined with hand stitches, sometimes it is worked just on its own. It has the same uses as hand embroidery, for decorating household linen, clothes—particularly children's clothes—or for making pictures or wall hangings, and so on. It can be used for appliqué, but here we are mainly concerned with stitches.

Machine embroidery shows up most clearly on a smooth surface, but it can also be used on slub fabrics which hand embroiderers find annoying to work on. If you want to use a soft or slippery fabric, tack tissue paper on to the bottom of it. This will help to keep it steady and the paper can easily be torn away when work is finished. Rayon and nylon and other very slippery fabrics are best avoided. Any material will pucker if the machine tension is too tight, though. Designs can be transferred to the fabric in the same ways as described on pages 50–51.

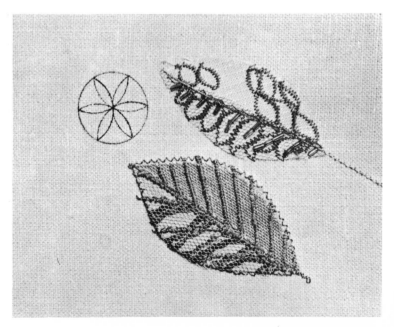

Example of embroidery worked on a modern sewing machine. Machine embroidery demands a different technique from hand embroidery but with practice it is possible to achieve fairly intricate designs.

Machine embroidery cotton comes in two thicknesses, No. 50 and No. 30; No. 50 is the finer. Ordinary mercerised cotton No. 40 used for dressmaking works perfectly well on lots of fabrics, but not those that are fine. In the machine you should have a size 11 needle for fine cotton and a size 14 for heavy cotton. Experiments can be made with other, thicker, threads. These are put on the spool while a No. 30 or 40 cotton is put in the needle. The embroidery has to be worked from the wrong side, so first the design line must be tacked on to the fabric, or a line of ordinary stitches worked on the right side first. *Coton à broder*, pearl cotton, crewel wool and floss silk can all be tried to see the effects they make. Aluminium threads and Lurex threads will add a sparkle—and work well in small quantities.

Borders and simple patterns

These can be worked with any machine. Borders make an attractive finish to place mats and other table linen, aprons, children's dresses, curtains and so on. They are excellent for a beginner to start with.

First try working a few straight lines, with varied widths between them, in different colours. Then try zig-zag lines, keeping the point of the needle in the fabric at each turn, and lifting the presser foot to swing fabric round. You can now work designs of diamonds or castellated patterns. Next work wavy lines: you can make a cable stitch similar to cable in knitting by crossing two wavy lines. This makes a particularly good pattern for experimenting with different thicknesses of thread and different fabrics.

Free embroidery

This can be worked only with a machine with a treadle or an electric model. Remove presser foot and put teeth out of action (if you haven't a knob for doing this you may have to buy a special plate to cover the teeth). The fabric to be embroidered must be placed inside a circular embroidery frame. The frames for machine embroideries are thinner than those for hand, and all have a screw for tightening them. The fabric should be held very taut in the frame. Thread the machine and put the frame under the needle then *lower presser foot lever*.

Start off by machining 2 or 3 stitches in same place to fasten threads, then you are free to move frame about as you like. Hold frame in both hands and move steadily as you operate machine. If you are a beginner it takes time to co-ordinate hand and leg movements, and a lot of practice to get used to the feel. Start by moving frame back and forth to make parallel horizontal lines. Lovely patterns can be created in this way, by altering the length of the stitches and varying the colour shades to build up a design it would take hours to work by hand.

Once you have got the idea, you can work vertical lines over the horizontal ones to make a darning pattern, then make loops and circles and finally follow design lines. Scrolls and circular movements can be worked very well in whip stitch. For this the top tension must be tightened and the spool tension loosened. A thinner thread goes in the spool. Hold frame in usual way and move slowly and evenly. The thick thread is completely covered by the thinner one underneath, creating fascinating effects.

Embroidery worked on an ordinary domestic sewing machine (no special embroidery stitch attachments).

Designs to make

In every pattern in this chapter specific thread and fabric colours are quoted. These are intended merely as a guide to the design we made up. The colours may, of course, be altered to suit personal preference, and the purpose for which the finished item is required.

A note concerning the USA equivalents for yarns, materials and needles quoted in the patterns is given on page 176.

Three wise men Christmas decoration

(making instructions begin on page 106)

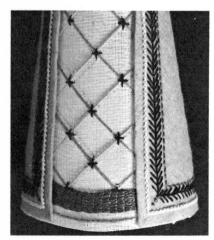

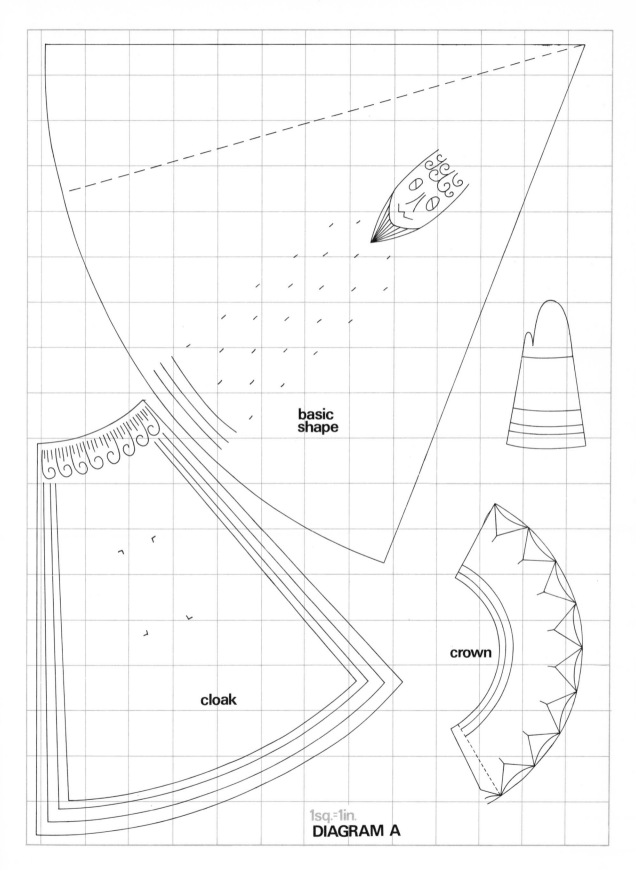

basic
shape

cloak

crown

1sq.=1in.
DIAGRAM A

STITCHES

Stem stitch
Satin stitch
Back stitch
Straight stitch
Cross stitch
Detached wheatear stitch (see below)
Laced running stitch
Fly stitch
Double knot stitch
French knots
Chain stitch
Buttonhole stitch

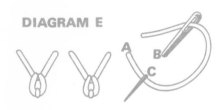

DIAGRAM E

MATERIALS

Of Clark's Anchor Stranded Cotton—1 skein each in Rose Pink 054/404, Parma Violet 0111/449, Jade 0188/524, Cobalt Blue 0133/510, Buttercup 0292/581, Peat Brown 0360/580, White 0402, and Black 0403. One piece each 12in. by 10in. of pink, purple and turquoise felt, and a small piece of black felt (for the face). ⅜yd. buckram or other stiff white material, 36in. wide. Small piece of iron-on bonded fibre interlining. 29 blue sequins. 35 gold sequins. 16 small pearls. 1 Milward 'Gold Seal' crewel needle No. 6.

DIAGRAMS

Diagram A (page 105) gives the basic shape of each king, the crown, cloak and gloves in a scaled-down version. Prepare a full-sized diagram as described for Beach Bag, page 120.

Diagram B gives a guide to the stitches and thread colours used to embroider king in purple felt (centre king in picture); **diagram C** gives a guide to the stitches and thread colours used to embroider king in pink felt (right-hand king in picture); **diagram D** gives a guide to the stitches and thread colours used to embroider king in turquoise felt (left-hand king in picture). (Diagrams B, C and D are on page 109.)

Diagram E shows how to work detached wheatear stitch: bring the thread through at A on diagram; insert needle a little to the right at B on diagram. Keeping the thread behind the needle, bring needle out at C; work a detached chain stitch.

TO MAKE

Note. Use 6 strands for laid threads; 3 strands for the rest of the embroidery.

Trace basic shape 3 times on to buckram; trace crown and cloak once and glove twice on to each colour of felt; trace face once only on to black felt. Cut round outer edges of all shapes: for purple crown cut on line A; for pink crown cut on line B; for turquoise crown cut on line C.

Now work the embroidery on the felt and buckram pieces, following stitch and colour key (page 109) and diagram B for purple king, diagram C for pink king, and diagram D for turquoise king. All unnumbered parts on the stitch and colour diagrams are worked in the same colour and stitch as the numbered parts most similar to them. Each glove is embroidered with the same border design as its matching cloak. The faces are worked in back stitch and stem stitch.

Stitch pearls and sequins in position, as indicated.

TO COMPLETE

Overlap the edges of the basic shape to the broken line as shown on diagram A (basic shape). Stab stitch to form a cone. Stitch black felt face in position to cone for purple king. Stitch gloves to matching cloaks, positioning ends of gloves on square marks as shown on diagram A (cloak). Stitch cloaks in position on cones. Cut 3 crown shapes from interlining and iron on to back of embroidered crowns. Overlap edges to the broken line and stitch. Place each crown in position on each king, and stitch round lower edge of crown to secure to king.

Couching and appliqué picture worked on a serge background.

Above: embroidered bridge cloth, worked mainly in stem, straight and satin stitches; Penelope Design P556. Right: 'Flower Tree' embroidered panel in an assortment of stitches, with stranded cotton, soft embroidery thread and tapestry wool; Penelope Design P541.

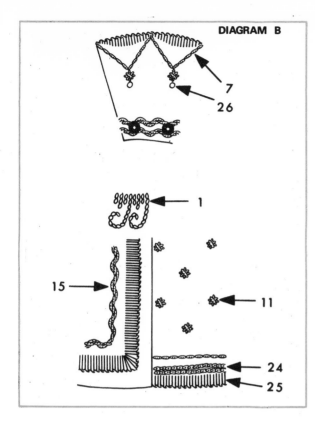

STITCH AND COLOUR KEY

1 White Stem stitch
2 Peat Brown Stem stitch
3 Black Stem stitch
4 Rose Pink Stem stitch
5 White Satin stitch
6 Cobalt Blue Satin stitch
7 Rose Pink Back stitch
8 Buttercup Back stitch
9 Jade Back stitch
10 Cobalt Blue Back stitch
11 Rose Pink Straight stitch stars
12 Black Cross stitch
13 Rose Pink Detached wheatear stitch
14 Cobalt Blue Detached wheatear stitch
15 Rose Pink Threaded running stitch
16 Black Fly stitch
17 White Double knot stitch
18 Cobalt Blue Double knot stitch
19 Rose Pink French knots
20 Jade French knots
21 Rose Pink Laid threads
22 Rose Pink Chain stitch
23 Jade Chain stitch
24 Parma Violet Chain stitch
25 Buttercup Buttonhole stitch
26 Pearls
27 Gold sequins
28 Blue sequins

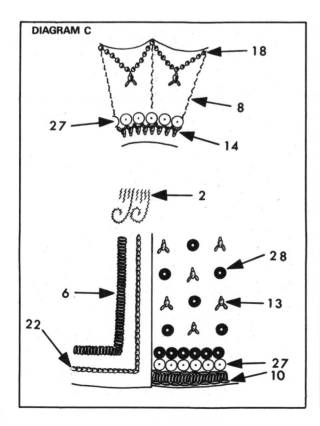

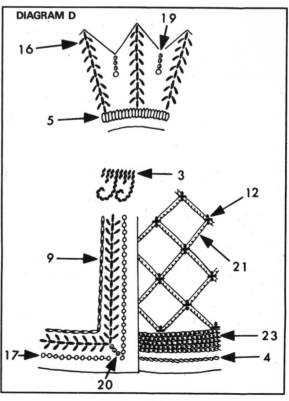

Scalloped cheval set

STITCHES
Stem stitch
Back stitch
Buttonhole stitch
Satin stitch

MATERIALS
6 skeins of Clark's Anchor Stranded Cotton in any shade wished. $\frac{3}{8}$yd. fine embroidery linen, 36in. wide, in a colour to tone or contrast with thread. 1 Milward 'Gold Seal' crewel needle No. 7.

DIAGRAMS

Diagram A gives a guide to the stitches used throughout.
Diagram B (page 112) gives a little over a quarter of the design for the big mat, and a quarter of the edging for each small mat, in a scaled-down version. Prepare a full-sized diagram as described for Beach Bag, page 120.

TO MAKE

Note. Use 3 strands throughout.
For large mat, cut a piece of linen measuring $13\frac{1}{2}$in. by 21in.
For each small mat, cut a piece of linen measuring $7\frac{1}{2}$in. square.
Fold each cut piece of linen in half both ways and crease lightly along folds. The broken lines on diagram B should coincide with the folds on the fabric pieces.
With one narrow end of large piece of fabric towards you, trace design from your prepared diagram on to lower left-hand quarter. Trace the right-hand side in reverse, omitting centre small motif (which overlaps fold). Trace upper half of design in a similar way.
Trace edging as given 4 times round each small piece of fabric to form a circle. Trace larger motif from design for large mat centrally on to each small mat.
Work embroidery following stitch key and diagram A. All unnumbered parts on the stitch diagram are worked in the same stitch as the numbered parts most similar to them.

TO COMPLETE

Press the embroidery carefully on the wrong side. The fabric beyond the buttonhole stitch edging is then cut away with sharp-pointed scissors. Cut from the wrong side, taking care not to snip the stitches.

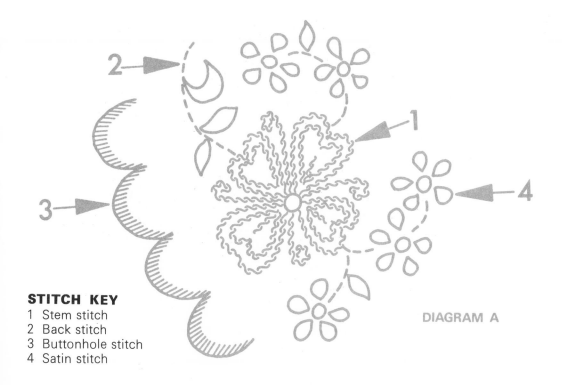

STITCH KEY
1 Stem stitch
2 Back stitch
3 Buttonhole stitch
4 Satin stitch

DIAGRAM A

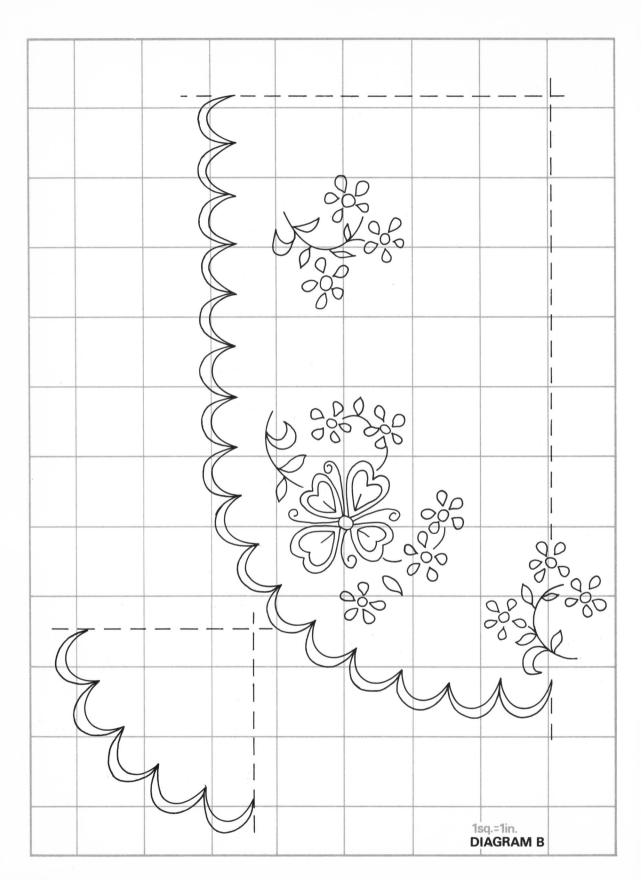

1sq.=1in.
DIAGRAM B

Shadow work dress

MATERIALS

Of Clark's Anchor Stranded Cotton—5 skeins Jade (medium) 0187/523, 3 skeins Jade (dark) 0189/525, and 2 skeins White 0402 (or any three contrasting or toning colours, as wished). A plain white nylon dress with full skirt (the dress used in our design has a taffeta underskirt, and the skirt is 2 yd. wide). 1 Milward 'Gold Seal' crewel needle No. 7.

STITCHES

Back stitch
Shadow work
Satin stitch

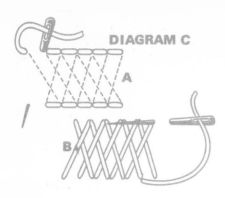

DIAGRAM C

DIAGRAMS

Diagram A gives a repeat of the design in actual size. The dotted lines at right of diagram indicate the way one repeat is linked to the next.

Diagram B gives a guide to the stitches and thread colours used throughout the design.

Diagram C shows 2 methods of working shadow work: in fig. 1 stitches are being worked on the right side of fabric—a small back stitch is worked alternately on each side of the traced double lines (the dotted lines on the diagram show the formation of the thread at the back of work). The colour of the thread appears delicately through the fabric. Fig. 2 shows the stitch worked on the wrong side of fabric as a closed herringbone stitch, with no spaces left between the stitches. Both methods achieve the same result.

TO MAKE

Note. Use 2 strands throughout.

Trace the motif on to skirt of dress, positioning it as wished, and linking motifs to form a continuous line (for the dress in our design, 24 repeats of the motif were used).

Work embroidery following stitch and colour key and diagram B. All unnumbered parts on the stitch and colour diagram are worked in the same stitch and colour as the numbered parts most similar to them.

TO COMPLETE

Press work lightly on the wrong side.

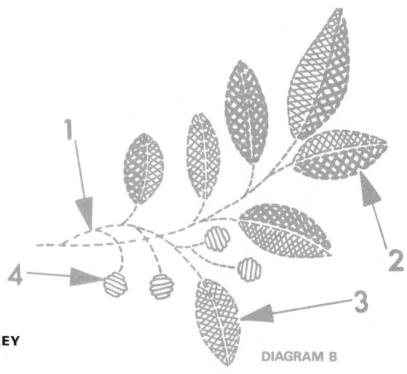

DIAGRAM B

STITCH AND COLOUR KEY

1 Medium Jade Back stitch
2 Dark Jade Shadow work
3 Medium Jade Shadow work
4 White Satin stitch

DIAGRAM A

Tablecloth

MATERIALS
Of Clark's Anchor Stranded Cotton—4 skeins Muscat Green 0280/948, 2 skeins Indigo 0125/533, 2 skeins Jade 0189/525, and 1 skein Spring Green 0239/778. $1\frac{1}{4}$yd. fine white embroidery linen, 45in. wide. 1 Milward 'Gold Seal' crewel needle No. 7.

STITCHES

Stem stitch	Straight stitch
Back stitch	Buttonhole stitch
French knots	Blanket stitch
Four-sided stitch	Chain stitch
	Interlaced band (see below)

DIAGRAMS

Diagram A gives a guide to the stitches and thread colours used·throughout the design.

Diagram B (page 118) gives a quarter of the design in a scaled-down version. Prepare a full-sized diagram as described for ·Beach Bag, page 120.

Diagram C shows how to work interlaced band stitch: this stitch is composed of 2 rows of back stitch with an interlacing. Work 2 parallel rows of back stitch, as shown in the diagram having the rows the required distance apart, with the stitches worked as on the diagram: i.e. the end of one stitch is directly in line with the centre of the opposite stitch. Bring the thread through at A and interlace it through every stitch.

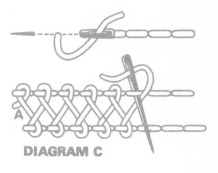

DIAGRAM C

TO MAKE

Note. Use 3 strands of thread throughout.

Fold the fabric in half both ways and crease lightly to mark fold lines. The broken lines on diagram B indicate the centre folds of the fabric. Trace design from your prepared diagram on to the lower right-hand quarter of fabric, repeat on other three quarters in a similar way.

Now work embroidery following stitch and colour key and diagram A. All unnumbered parts on the stitch and thread diagram are worked in the same stitch as the numbered parts most similar to them.

TO COMPLETE

Turn back 1-in. hems on all edges, mitre corners and slip-stitch neatly. Press the embroidery on the wrong side.

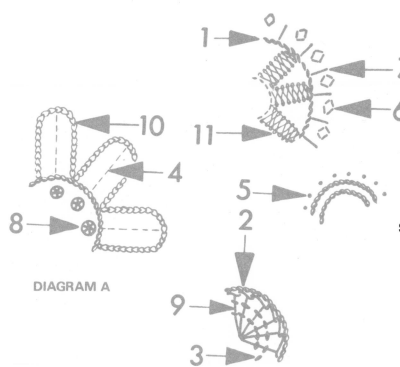

DIAGRAM A

STITCH AND COLOUR KEY

1. Indigo Stem stitch
2. Spring Green Stem stitch
3. Indigo Back stitch
4. Muscat Green Back stitch
5. Indigo French knots
6. Jade Four-sided stitch
7. Jade Straight stitch
8. Jade Buttonhole stitch
9. Jade Blanket stitch
10. Muscat Green Chain stitch
11. Muscat Green Interlaced band

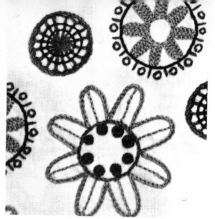

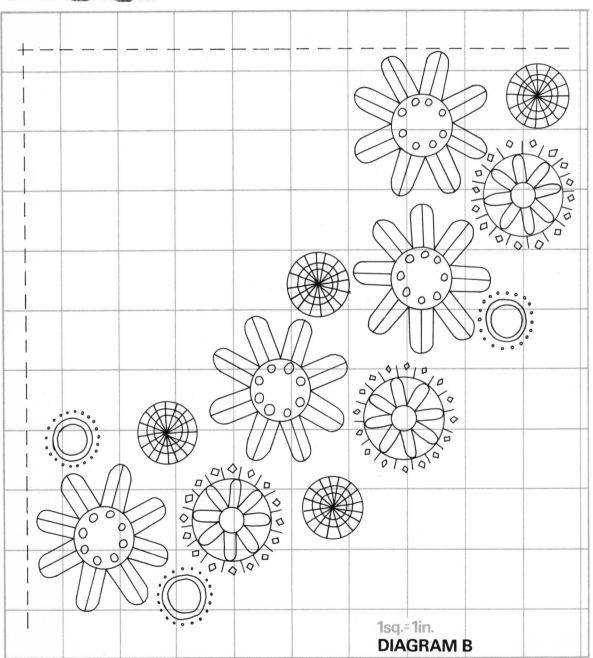

1sq.=1in.
DIAGRAM B

Beach bag

MATERIALS

Of Coats Anchor Tapisserie Wool—1 skein each in Kingfisher, shades 0162 (medium) and 0164 (dark), Amber Gold 0306, Coffee 0381, Terra Cotta 0339, and White 0402. $\frac{1}{2}$yd. biscuit-coloured mediumweight embroidery linen, 50in. wide, or other similar mediumweight fabric. $\frac{5}{8}$yd. plastic material, 36in. wide, for lining. 1yd. firm fabric, 36in. wide, for interlining. 3yd. heavy cord for handles. Piece of cardboard for base. 1 reel Coats Satinised/Super Sheen No. 40 to match fabric. 1 Milward 'Gold Seal' chenille needle No. 19.

STITCHES

Stem stitch
Satin stitch
Straight stitch
Couching
Fly stitch
Roumanian stitch

DIAGRAMS

Diagram A gives a scaled-down version of the complete design. Each square on the diagram represents 1in. On a large sheet of strong white paper carefully rule and mark out a grid of 1-in. squares. Now carefully copy the outlines from our scaled-down diagram on to your prepared grid, matching position of shapes, angles and curves in relation to the grid lines as accurately as possible. When you are satisfied your diagram is correct, go over it again with a dark pencil, or waterproof Indian ink.

Diagram B gives a guide to the stitches and thread colours used throughout the design.

TO MAKE

Note. $\frac{1}{2}$-in. turnings allowed on all seams.
From both linen and interlining, cut one piece 17in. by 36in. for main section, and 2 pieces each 4in. by 17in. for side gussets.

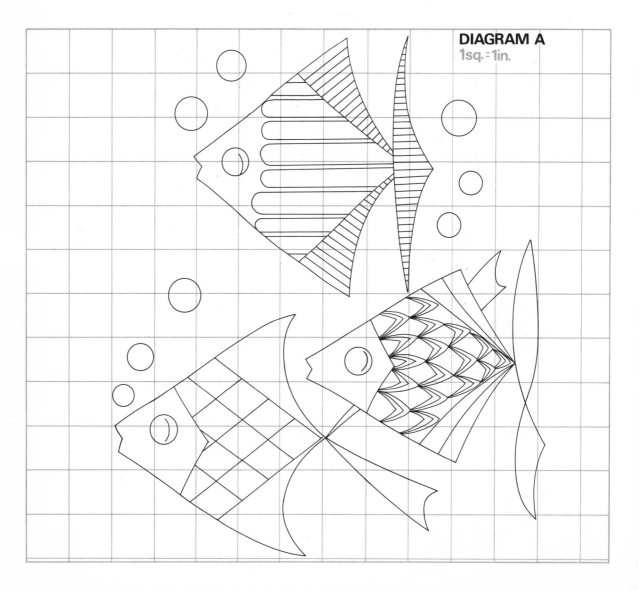

DIAGRAM A
1sq.=1in.

From plastic, cut one piece 17in. by 33in. and 2 pieces each 4in. by 15½in.

Trace design from your prepared drawing on to linen, starting tracing 3in. from one short end on main section.

Work embroidery following stitch and colour key and diagram B. All unnumbered parts on the stitch and thread diagram are worked in the same stitch and colour as the numbered parts most similar to them.

TO COMPLETE

Press the embroidery on the wrong side.

To make up, pin interlining to linen and, with right sides together, machine stitch side gussets in position. Cut a piece from cardboard 3in. by 16in. and herringbone stitch to interlining to form a base. Turn down 1½in. on top edge and herringbone stitch to interlining. Turn to right side. Make up plastic lining and insert into bag, wrong sides together. Turn in ½in. on top edges and hem to linen. Join ends of cord and sew to bag, 1¼in. from gusset seam, as shown in photograph on page 119.

STITCH AND COLOUR KEY

1 White Stem stitch
2 Terra Cotta Stem stitch
3 Medium Kingfisher Stem stitch
4. Dark Kingfisher Stem stitch
5 Coffee Stem stitch
6 White Satin stitch
7 Amber Gold Satin stitch
8 Terra Cotta Satin stitch
9 Medium Kingfisher Satin stitch
10 Coffee Satin stitch
11 Amber Gold Straight stitch
12 White Couching
13 Amber Gold Couching
14 Terra Cotta Couching
15 Medium Kingfisher Couching
16 Coffee Couching
17 Amber Gold Fly stitch
18 Medium Kingfisher Fly stitch
19 Dark Kingfisher Roumanian stitch

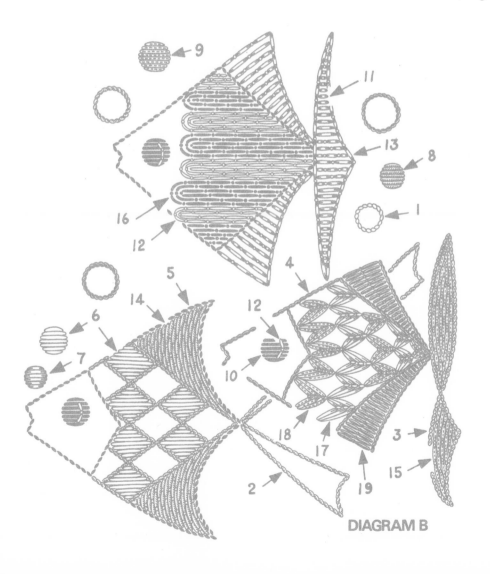

DIAGRAM B

Nursery motif

STITCHES
Double knot stitch
Straight stitch
Stem stitch
Satin stitch
Fly stitch
French knots
Running stitch
Detached chain stitch

MATERIALS
Of Clark's Anchor Stranded Cotton—1 skein each in White 0402, Scarlet 046/469, and Jade 0188/524 (or any three shades as wished). 1 shirt or suit in a colour to contrast or tone with thread colours (the suit in our design is dark green). 1 Milward 'Gold Seal' crewel needle No. 6.

DIAGRAMS

Diagram A gives the complete motif in actual size.
Diagram B gives a guide to the stitches and thread colours used throughout the design.

TO MAKE

Note. Use 3 strands for double knot stitch; 2 strands for the rest of the embroidery.

Trace the motif as given in diagram A on to shirt, positioning it as wished.

Work embroidery, following stitch and colour key, and diagram B. All unnumbered parts on the stitch and thread diagram are worked in the same colour and stitch as the numbered parts most similar to them.

TO COMPLETE

Press embroidery on the wrong side.

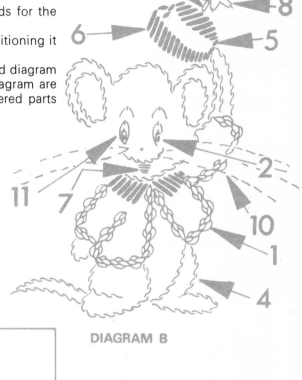

DIAGRAM B

DIAGRAM A

STITCH AND COLOUR KEY

1 Jade Double knot stitch
2 Scarlet Straight stitch
3 Jade Straight stitch
4 White Stem stitch
5 Scarlet Stem stitch
6 Scarlet Satin stitch
7 White Satin stitch
8 White Fly stitch
9 White French knots
10 White Running stitch
11 White Detached chain stitch

Cutwork
table mat

(making instructions begin on page 127)

MATERIALS
Of Clark's Anchor Pearl Cotton No. 8 (10-gram ball)—2 balls White 0402, and 1 ball Peacock Blue 0169/874 (or any two contrasting shades). Alternatively use Clark's Anchor Stranded Cotton—8 skeins of White 0402, 2 skeins Peacock Blue 0169/874. $\frac{3}{4}$yd. fine embroidery linen, 36in. wide. 1 Milward 'Gold Seal' crewel needle No. 6.

STITCHES
Stem stitch
Buttonhole stitch
Satin stitch

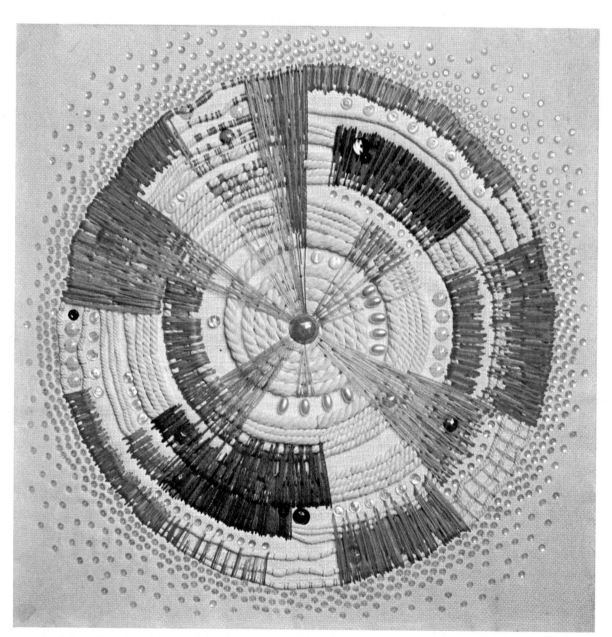

A colourful modern design incorporating couched piping cord.

Right: 'A Partridge in a Pear Tree', an embroidered panel worked in an assortment of stitches and couched threads; Penelope Design P203.
Below: 'Bouquet', another embroidered panel, also with an assortment of stitches and couched threads; Penelope Design P519.

DIAGRAMS

Diagram A gives a guide to the stitches and thread colours used throughout the design.

Diagram B (page 128) gives one section of the design in a scaled-down version. Prepare a full-sized diagram as described for Beach Bag, page 120.

TO MAKE

Note. Use 3 strands throughout.

Cut one piece from fabric measuring 27in. square. Fold across the centre both ways and diagonally both ways and crease lightly to mark these folds. The straight broken lines on diagram B indicate a diagonal fold and a centre fold.

Trace the given section of the design positioning the design so the fold lines on the fabric line up with the broken lines on the diagram. To complete the circle trace section 5 more times, linking sections as indicated by small broken outlines.

Work embroidery, following the stitch and colour key and diagram A. All unnumbered parts on the stitch and colour diagram are worked in the same colour and stitch as the numbered parts most similar to them.

TO COMPLETE

Press the embroidery on the wrong side. Cut away all parts of fabric marked 'X' on diagram B, and also the surplus fabric round the outer edge using small sharp-pointed scissors. Take care not to snip the buttonhole stitching.

STITCH AND COLOUR KEY

1 Peacock Blue Stem stitch
2 White Buttonhole stitch
3 Peacock Blue Satin stitch

DIAGRAM A

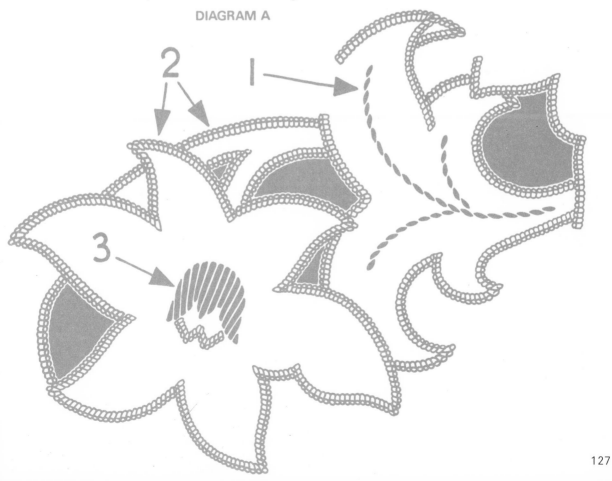

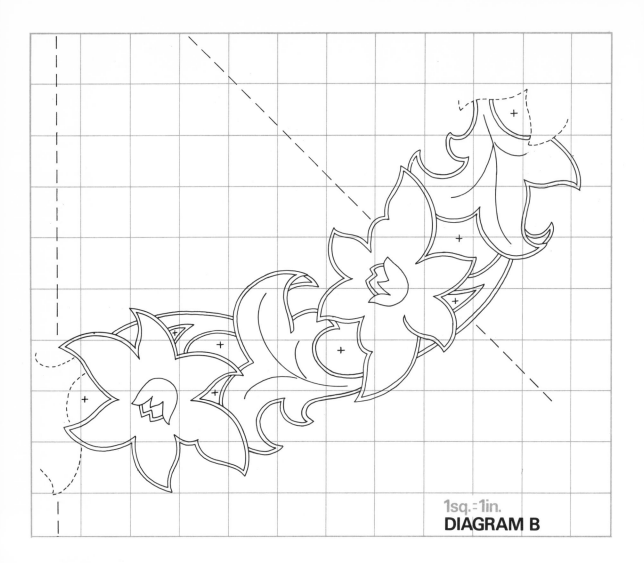

1sq.=1in.
DIAGRAM B

Drawn-fabric chairback

MATERIALS
3 skeins Clark's Anchor Stranded Cotton in any shade wished (our design uses Linen shade 0392). $\frac{3}{4}$yd. evenweave embroidery linen, 22in. wide, 28 threads to 1in. 1 Milward 'Gold Seal' tapestry needle No. 24.

STITCHES
Cable stitch
Straight stitch
Diagonal raised band

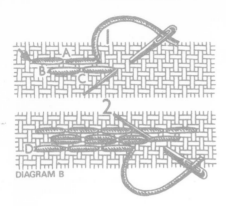

DIAGRAM B

DIAGRAMS
Diagram A shows the arrangement of the stitches on the threads of the fabric. Each of the small background squares on the diagram represents one thread of the fabric. Right-hand end of top section diagram joins on to left-hand end of bottom section, as indicated by arrows. This complete section represents the lower right-hand quarter of the complete design.

Diagram B (1 and 2) shows how to work cable stitch: this stitch is worked from left to right. Bring the thread out at the arrow on fig. 1, insert the needle at A (4 threads to the right), bring the needle out at B (1 thread down and 2 threads to the left), insert the needle at C (4 threads to the right), and bring out at A. Continue in this way to the end of the row. Commence the 2nd row at D (2 threads below the first stitch of the previous row) and work in a similar way, but working the top stitches into same holes as lower stitches of previous row (fig. 2).

TO MAKE
Note. Use 3 strands throughout.
Trim fabric to $17\frac{1}{2}$in. by 27in. Mark the centre lengthwise with a line of basting stitches. The blank arrow on diagram A should coincide with the basting stitches on your fabric.
With one short side of fabric towards you, begin embroidery $5\frac{1}{2}$in. up from lower edge, and starting with cable stitch at point marked with blank arrow on diagram. Follow diagram and stitch key, pulling each stitch firmly as you work it.
Complete work on the quarter of the design given, then work design in reverse from blank arrow to complete lower half of the design. In a similar way, work upper half of the design, leaving 6 threads between upper and lower halves.

TO COMPLETE
Turn back a 2-in. hem along lower edge (the edge nearest to embroidery), and $\frac{1}{2}$in. along other 3 edges. Mitre corners and slipstitch neatly round all edges.

STITCH KEY
1 Cable stitch
2 Straight stitch
3 Diagonal raised band

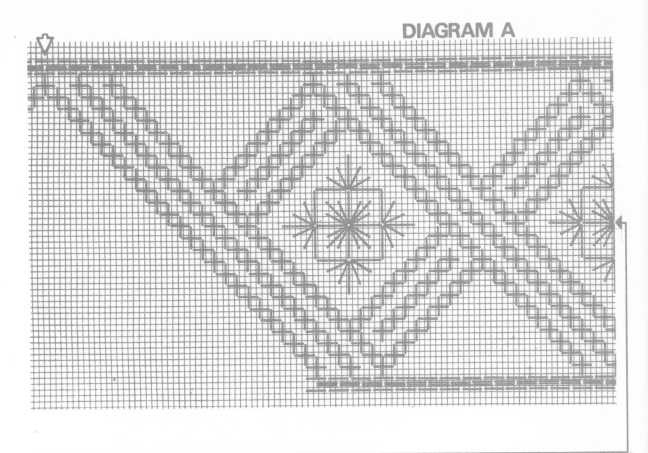

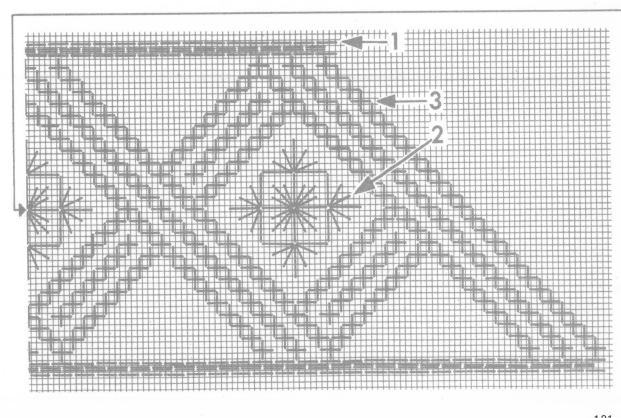

Cross stitch runner

MATERIALS

Of Clark's Anchor Stranded Cotton—3 skeins each of Jade 0188, and White 0402, 2 skeins of Black 0403 (or any three shades as wished). $\frac{1}{2}$yd. mediumweight evenweave embroidery linen, 59in. wide, 21 threads to 1in., in a colour to tone or contrast with thread shades (we used a red linen for our design). 1 Milward 'Gold Seal' tapestry needle No. 24.

STITCH
Cross stitch

DIAGRAM
Diagram A (page 134) shows arrangement of stitches on threads of the fabric. Each of the small background squares on the diagram represents 3 threads of the fabric. The section of the design shown represents one quarter of the complete design.

TO MAKE
Note. Use 4 strands throughout.
Cut a piece from fabric $31\frac{1}{2}$in. by $15\frac{1}{2}$in. Mark the centre both ways with a line of basting stitches. The black arrows on the diagram should coincide with the basting stitches on your fabric.
The embroidery is worked throughout in cross stitch. Begin work with one long side of fabric facing you, starting the design centrally and working the quarter as given on the diagram. Follow colour key on page 134. Work other three quarters of the design to correspond.

TO COMPLETE
Press the embroidery on the wrong side. Turn back $\frac{1}{2}$-in. hems round all edges, mitre corners, and slipstitch neatly in place.

DIAGRAM A

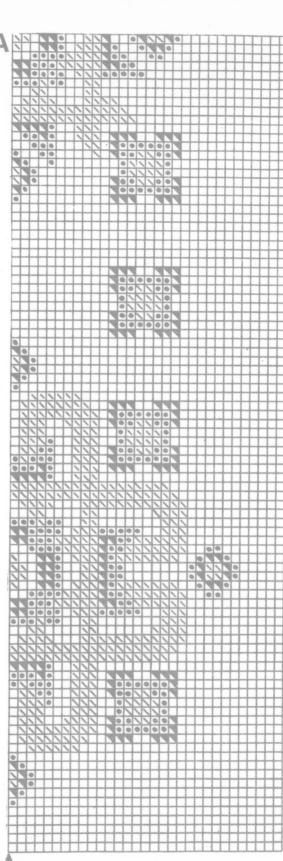

COLOUR KEY

 Jade

 White

 Black

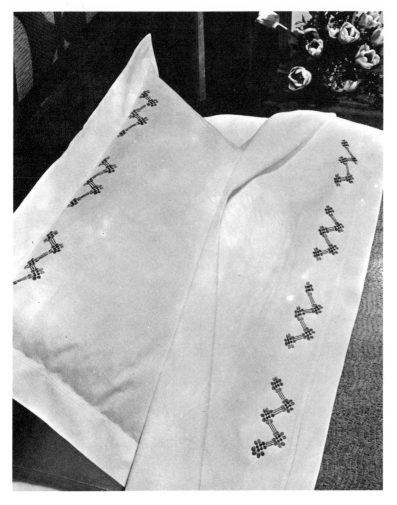

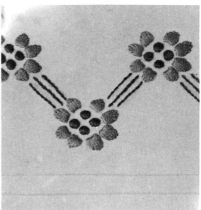

Sheet and pillowcase

STITCHES
Detached chain stitch
Back stitch
Satin stitch

MATERIALS
Of Clark's Anchor Stranded Cotton—3 skeins Delphinium (medium blue) 0121, and 2 skeins Delphinium (dark blue) 0123. A white or plain pastel-coloured sheet and matching pillowcase. 1 Milward 'Gold Seal' crewel needle No. 7.

DIAGRAMS
Diagram A (page 136) gives one complete motif in actual size.
Diagram B (page 136) gives a guide to the stitches and thread colours used throughout the design.

TO MAKE
Note. Use 2 strands of medium blue throughout the design, 3 strands of dark blue.
Fold sheet in half lengthwise, and fold pillowcase in half widthwise. Crease lightly to mark folds. The broken line on diagram A indicates the centre folds.
Trace motif on to the sheet, making first tracing centrally across fold (line up broken line on diagram with your fold line) and $2\frac{1}{4}$in. down from top edge of sheet. Trace the motif 4 times more, to give 2 motifs on either side of the central motif (total of 5 motifs altogether), spacing motifs $2\frac{1}{2}$in. apart.

If using a double bed size sheet you may wish to add another motif to each side.

Trace motif on to pillowcase, making first tracing centrally across fold (line up broken line on diagram with your fold line) and $2\frac{3}{4}$in. down from top edge of pillowcase. Trace the motif twice more—one on either side of the central motif, spacing motifs $2\frac{1}{2}$in. apart.

Work embroidery following stitch and colour key and diagram B. All unnumbered parts on the stitch and colour diagram are worked in the same stitch and colour as the numbered parts most similar to them.

TO COMPLETE
Press embroidery on the wrong side.

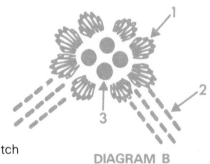

DIAGRAM B

STITCH AND COLOUR KEY
1 Medium Blue Detached chain stitch
2 Dark Blue Back stitch
3 Dark Blue Satin stitch

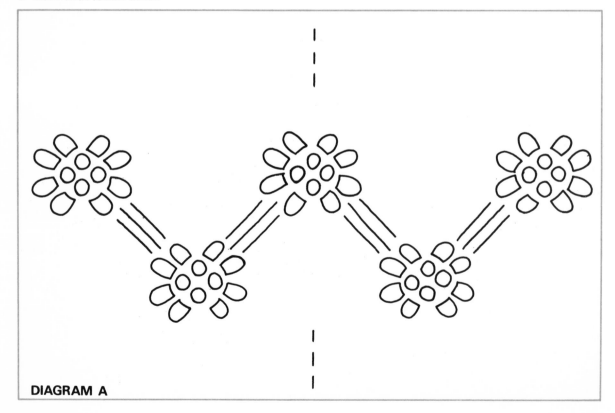

DIAGRAM A

MATERIALS

To make 4 mats : of Clark's Anchor Stranded Cotton—2 skeins Cinnamon (dark) 0371/672, 1 skein each of Gorse Yellow 0301/442, Amber Gold 0307/733, Tangerine 0311/512, Cinnamon (medium) 0369/477, Cinnamon (light) 0368/476 and Muscat Green 0280/948. $\frac{3}{4}$yd. fine embroidery linen, 36in. wide. 1 reel Coats Satinised/Super Sheen No. 40 to match fabric. 1 Milward 'Gold Seal' crewel needle No. 6.

STITCHES

Long and short stitch	Satin stitch
Back stitch	Double knot stitch
Stem stitch	French knots

Table mats

DIAGRAMS

Diagram A gives one motif of the design in actual size.
Diagram B gives a guide to the stitches and thread colours used throughout the design.

TO MAKE

Note. Use 3 strands throughout.

Cut 4 pieces from fabric, each 18in. by 12½in. Fold each piece across the centre widthwise and crease lightly to mark fold line. With one long side towards you, trace motif centrally on to fold, and positioning lowest point of motif 1½in. up from lower edge of fabric. Trace motif 4 more times—twice on the right of central motif, twice on the left. Position motifs so the lower line of each just touches the lower line of the motif next to it. Work embroidery following stitch and colour key and diagram B. All unnumbered parts of the stitch and colour diagram are worked in the same stitch and colour as the numbered parts most similar to them.

TO COMPLETE

Press the embroidery on the wrong side. Turn in ½-in. hems round all edges, mitre corners and slipstitch neatly in place.

STITCH AND COLOUR KEY

1 Tangerine Long and short stitch
2 Gorse Yellow Long and short stitch
3 Amber Gold Long and short stitch
4 Gorse Yellow Back stitch
5 Tangerine Stem stitch
6 Cinnamon (medium) Stem stitch
7 Cinnamon (light) Stem stitch
8 Muscat Green Satin stitch
9 Cinnamon (dark) Double knot stitch
10 Amber Gold French knots

DIAGRAM A

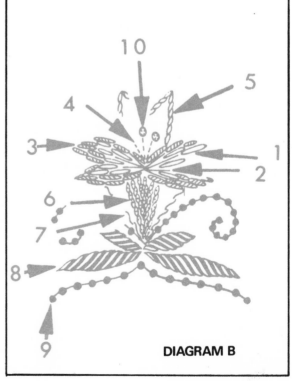

DIAGRAM B

Long runner

MATERIALS

Of Coats Anchor Tapisserie Wool—1 skein each of Cyclamen 085, Violet 095, Canary Yellow 0288, and Raspberry 0871, 2 skeins of Grass Green 0246. $\frac{3}{8}$yd. mediumweight embroidery linen, 48in. wide, in green or colour wished. 1 reel Coats Satinised/Super Sheen No. 40 to match fabric. 1 Milward 'Gold Seal' tapestry needle No. 19.

STITCHES

Straight stitch
Stem stitch
Satin stitch
French knots

DIAGRAMS

Diagram A gives a guide to the stitches and thread colours used throughout the design.

Diagram B gives one section of the complete design in a scaled-down version. Prepare a full-sized diagram as described for Beach Bag, page 120.

TO MAKE

Cut one piece from fabric $43\frac{1}{2}$in. by $12\frac{1}{2}$in. Fold fabric across the centre both ways and crease lightly to mark. From your prepared diagram trace the big circular flower motif only centrally on to fabric. Then trace the complete section of the design as given on the diagram on to the right-hand side of fabric, keeping the centre of the big circular flower on the lengthwise fold of fabric, and the broken outline on the diagram coinciding with the motif already traced. Turn fabric and trace other half of design to correspond. Now work embroidery, following stitch and colour key and diagram A.

All unnumbered parts on the stitch and colour diagram are worked in the same stitch and colour as the numbered parts most similar to them.

TO COMPLETE

Press embroidery on the wrong side. Turn in $\frac{1}{2}$-in. hems on all edges, mitre corners and slipstitch neatly in place.

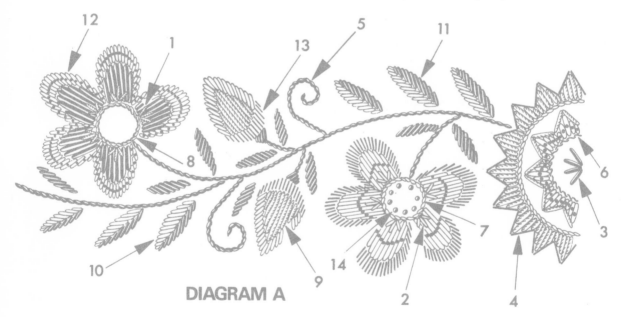

DIAGRAM A

STITCH AND COLOUR KEY

1 Cyclamen Straight stitch
2 Canary Yellow Straight stitch
3 Grass Green Straight stitch
4 Raspberry Straight stitch
5 Grass Green Stem stitch
6 Raspberry Stem stitch
7 Canary Yellow Stem stitch
8 Cyclamen Stem stitch
9 Cyclamen Satin stitch
10 Canary Yellow Satin stitch
11 Grass Green Satin stitch
12 Violet Satin stitch
13 Raspberry Satin stitch
14 Grass Green French knots

1sq.=1in.
DIAGRAM B

Umbrella cover

(making instructions begin on page 145)

STITCHES
Double knot stitch
Satin stitch
Chain stitch
Stem stitch
Couched fly stitch
French knots

MATERIALS
1 skein of Clark's Anchor Stranded Cotton in chosen colour. ¼yd. nylon or other suitable fabric, 36in. wide, in a colour to tone or contrast with thread shade (we used a white nylon fabric with embroidery worked in Black shade 0403). A 4-in. zip fastener to match fabric colour. 1 reel Coats Gossamer/Drima to match fabric. 1 Milward 'Gold Seal' crewel needle No. 6.

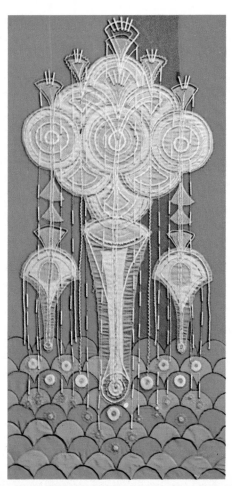

Left: 'The Fountain', a formal design with simple couching and appliqué.
Bottom of page: 'Gold Development', a machine embroidery.
Below: 'Firmament', another machine embroidery.

Above: a modern machine embroidery.
Right: Florentine table mats (for
making instructions, see page 167).

DIAGRAMS
Diagram A (page 146) gives one half of the complete design in actual size (one large and one small motif).
Diagram B (page 146) gives a guide to the stitches used throughout the design.

TO MAKE
Note. Use 2 strands to work small motifs, 3 strands for large.
Cut one piece from fabric 13in. by 9in. for main section.
Cut strip measuring 9in. by 5½in. for cuff of cover.
Fold main section in half across the centre widthwise and crease lightly to mark the fold line.
The broken line on diagram A indicates the centre fold of the fabric. Trace the motif as given in diagram A centrally on to your fabric so the broken line on diagram coincides with your fold line. Turn fabric and repeat tracing for other half.
Now work embroidery following stitch key and diagram B.
All unnumbered parts on the stitch diagram are worked in the same stitch as the numbered parts most similar to them.

TO COMPLETE
Press the embroidery on the wrong side.
Place the embroidered fabric round the umbrella, wrong side out, and pin to shape so the cover fits snugly but not too tightly over the umbrella. Trim away excess fabric, leaving ½in. on each edge for seams. Remove fabric from umbrella. Turn up ¼-in. hem at lower edge, and stitch neatly. With right sides together and taking ½-in. turnings, stitch long seam, leaving 4in. unstitched at top for zip. Turn cover to right side, and stitch zip into opening. Fold cuff section in half lengthwise and trim to fit top edge of cover, allowing ¼in. at sides for seams. With right sides together and taking ¼in. turnings, stitch side seams of cuff. Turn to right side. With right sides together, pin cuff in place to cover, lining up opening in cover with side edges of cuff. Pin through single layer of cuff only. Baste then stitch. Turn in remaining raw edge of cuff and slipstitch in place to wrong side of seam just stitched.

STITCH KEY
1 Double knot stitch
2 Satin stitch
3 Chain stitch
4 Stem stitch
5 Couched fly stitch
6 French knots

DIAGRAM A

DIAGRAM B

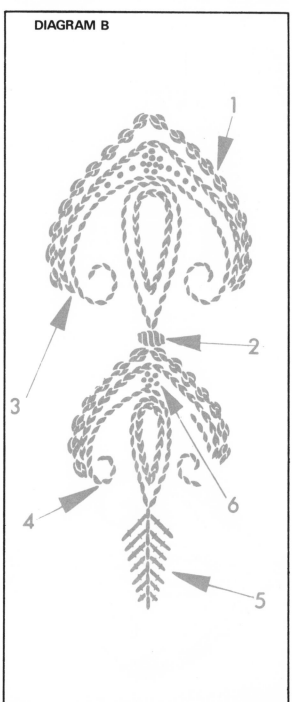

Cot sheet

MATERIALS
Of Clark's Anchor Stranded Cotton—1 skein each of Cerise (medium) 032, Cerise (dark) 035, Jade (light) 0185, Jade (medium) 0187, Buttercup 0297, and Tangerine 0314. A fine linen cot sheet in white or plain pastel shade. 1 Milward 'Gold Seal' crewel needle No. 7.

DIAGRAMS
Diagram A (page 148) gives a section of design in a scaled-down version. Prepare a full-sized diagram as described for Beach Bag, page 120.
Diagram B (page 148) gives a guide to stitches and thread colours.

TO MAKE
Note. Use 2 strands for small flower motifs, 3 strands for rest. Fold sheet in half lengthwise and crease lightly to mark fold line. With top edge of sheet towards you, trace the design from your prepared diagram, positioning the flower motif from left of elephants on the centre fold of your sheet, and $5\frac{1}{2}$in. down from top edge of sheet. Trace design in reverse from centre motif on to left-hand side of sheet.
Work embroidery following stitch and colour key and diagram B. All unnumbered parts on the stitch and colour diagram are worked in the same stitch and colour as the numbered parts most similar to them. Reverse the colour scheme in the motifs on the left-hand side.

TO COMPLETE
Press the embroidery on the wrong side.

STITCHES
Stem stitch
Back stitch
Satin stitch
Detached chain stitch
Fly stitch

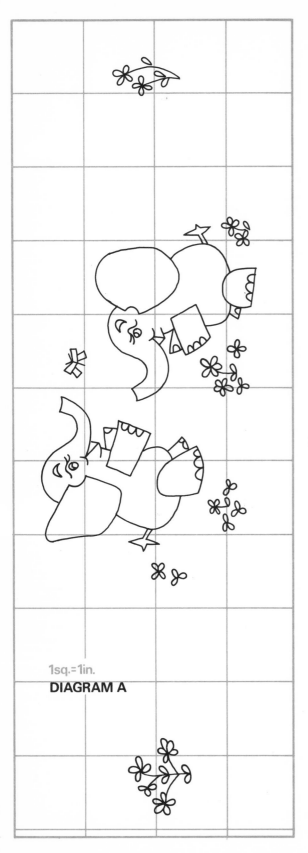

1sq.=1in.
DIAGRAM A

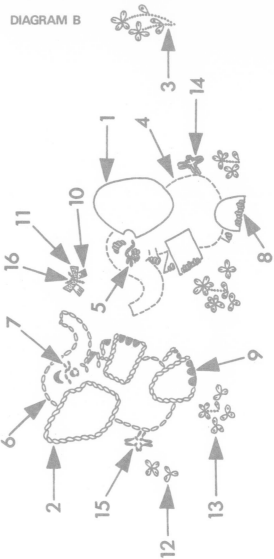

DIAGRAM B

STITCH AND COLOUR KEY

1 Medium Cerise Stem stitch
2 Light Jade Stem stitch
3 Tangerine Stem stitch
4 Medium Cerise Back stitch
5 Dark Cerise Back stitch
6 Light Jade Back stitch
7 Medium Jade Back stitch
8 Dark Cerise Satin stitch
9 Medium Jade Satin stitch
10 Buttercup Satin stitch
11 Tangerine Satin stitch
12 Buttercup Detached chain stitch
13 Tangerine Detached chain stitch
14 Dark Cerise Fly stitch
15 Medium Jade Fly stitch
16 Tangerine Fly stitch

Bible cover

MATERIALS

For a cover to fit a Bible approximately 6½in. by 4½in. by 1½in.. of Clark's Anchor Stranded Cotton—1 skein each Gold (pale) 0885/Spec. 9384, Gold (medium) 0887/Spec. 9386, and Brown 0889/Spec. 9388. ¼yd. blue cotton (or colour required) or other suitable fabric, 36in. wide. Piece of bonded fibre iron-on interlining 10½in. by 6½in. 1 reel Coats Satinised/Super Sheen No. 40 to match fabric. 1yd. fine blue cord. 1 Milward 'Gold Seal' crewel needle No. 7.

STITCHES

Stem stitch
Back stitch
Satin stitch
Couching
Straight stitch
Double knot stitch

DIAGRAMS
Diagram A gives complete design in actual size.
Diagram B gives a guide to the stitches and thread colours used throughout the design.

TO MAKE
Note. Use 2 strands throughout.
Cut 2 pieces from fabric, each 8in. by 18in. One piece will be the outside of cover, the other will be used as a lining. Iron inter-lining centrally on to the wrong side of one piece of fabric. With one long side of this interlined piece of fabric towards you and right side up, trace design from diagram A centrally on to fabric, $4\frac{3}{4}$in. from the right-hand side edge. Work embroidery following stitch and colour key and diagram B. All unnumbered parts on the stitch and colour diagram are worked in the same stitch and colour as the numbered parts most similar to them.

TO COMPLETE
Press embroidery on the wrong side. Turn $\frac{3}{4}$in. to wrong side round all edges of embroidered piece, mitre corners and herring-bone stitch lightly to hold in position. Turn in 1in. round all edges of lining piece, and place lining centrally to embroidered fabric, wrong sides together. Slipstitch neatly in place. Turn back 3in. on side edges to form flaps. Slipstitch upper and lower edges of flaps. Stitch cord in position round outer edges of cover, as shown in photograph on page 149.

STITCH AND COLOUR KEY

1	Medium Gold Stem stitch	6	Brown Satin stitch
2	Brown Stem stitch	7	Medium Gold Couching
3	Pale Gold Stem stitch	8	Medium Gold Straight stitch
4	Medium Gold Back stitch	9	Medium Gold Double knot stitch
5	Pale Gold Back stitch	10	Pale Gold Double knot stitch

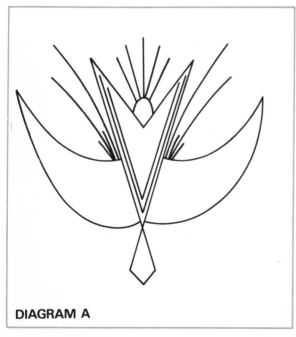

DIAGRAM A

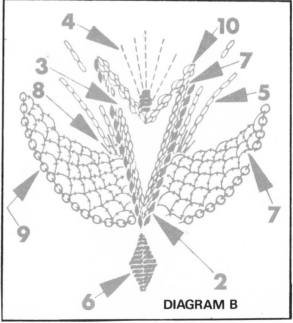

DIAGRAM B

MATERIALS

Of Clark's Anchor Stranded Cotton—1 skein each of Peacock Blue 0170/875, Jade 0189/525, Viridian 0230/943, and Spring Green 0239/778. $\frac{1}{4}$yd. grey mediumweight embroidery linen, 48in. wide $\frac{1}{8}$yd. green felt, 36in. wide, $\frac{1}{8}$yd. heavyweight bonded fibre interlining, 32in. wide. 1 reel Coats Satinised/Super Sheen No. 40. 1 Milward 'Gold Seal' crewel needle No. 7.

DIAGRAMS

Diagram A (page 152) gives design in a scaled-down version. Prepare a full-sized diagram as described for Beach Bag, page 120. The broken line round the design indicates the finished shape of the spectacle case. For the compact cover, only one of the 3 motifs is used—whichever one you prefer.
Diagram B (page 152) gives a guide to stitches and thread colours.

TO MAKE

Note. Use 3 strands throughout.
To make a spectacle case. From linen cut 2 pieces, each 7$\frac{1}{2}$in. by 3$\frac{1}{2}$in. Trace design from your prepared diagram centrally on to one piece of linen.

Spectacle case and compact cover

STITCHES

Stem stitch
Fly stitch
French knots
Chain stitch
Buttonhole stitch
Back stitch

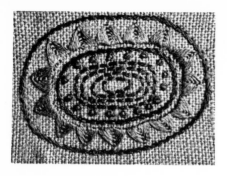

Work embroidery, following stitch and colour key and diagram B. All unnumbered parts on the stitch and colour diagram are worked in the same stitch and colour as the numbered parts most similar to them.

To make compact cover. From linen cut 2 pieces, each 4in. by 3½in. Trace one motif from your prepared diagram centrally on to one piece of linen. Work embroidery as for spectacle case.

TO COMPLETE

Press embroidery on the wrong side.

Spectacle case. Cut 2 pieces from interlining following broken outline on diagram A. Place one piece centrally on wrong side of embroidered fabric and trim to ¼in. from interlining. Turn this allowance to inside and herringbone stitch to interlining. Cut felt slightly smaller than embroidered piece and slipstitch to wrong side. Make up other side of case in a similar way. Slipstitch the 2 sides together, leaving top edges open so spectacles may be inserted easily.

Compact cover. Cut 2 pieces from interlining, each 3½in. by 3in. Make up in a similar way as for spectacle case.

STITCH AND COLOUR KEY

1 Peacock Blue Stem stitch
2 Viridian Stem stitch
3 Spring Green Stem stitch
4 Jade Fly stitch
5 Viridian Fly stitch
6 Spring Green Fly stitch
7 Peacock Blue French knots
8 Jade French knots
9 Spring Green French knots
10 Peacock Blue Chain stitch
11 Spring Green Chain stitch
12 Peacock Blue Buttonhole stitch
13 Viridian Back stitch

1sq.=1in.
DIAGRAM A

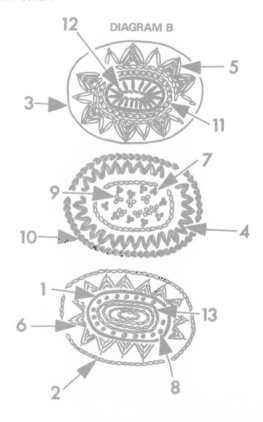

DIAGRAM B

MATERIALS

Of Clark's Anchor Tapisserie Wool—2 skeins each of Cyclamen 089 and White 0402, 1 skein of Black 0403. Of Clark's Anchor Stranded Cotton—2 skeins each of Cyclamen 089 and Black 0403, 1 skein of White 0402. 1yd. mediumweight turquoise blue slub linen furnishing fabric, 48in. wide (or colour required). ¾yd. black towelling, 36in. wide, or other similar fabric for backing bath mat. 1 piece foam filling, 20in. by 30in., ½in. thick, or other suitable material for interlining bath mat. ¾yd. elastic for toilet seat cover. 1 each Milward 'Gold Seal' crewel needle No. 6 for stranded cotton, and a chenille needle No. 19 for tapisserie wool.

DIAGRAMS

Diagram A (page 154) gives a guide to the stitches and thread colours used throughout the design.

Diagram B (page 155) gives a scaled-down version of a section of the design. Each square represents 1in. On a sheet of white paper measuring about 20in. by 15in., rule and mark out a grid of 1-in. squares. Now carefully copy the outlines from our scaled-down diagram on to your prepared grid, matching position of shapes, angles and curves in relation to the grid lines as accurately as possible. When you are satisfied your diagram is correct, go over it again with a dark pencil, or waterproof Indian ink.

TO MAKE

Note. Use 3 strands of stranded cotton throughout, and match stranded cotton to tapisserie wool for tying stitch in couching.

To make bath mat. Cut one piece from turquoise fabric 20in. by 30in. Fold fabric diagonally both ways from corner to corner and crease lightly to mark these fold lines. The broken lines on diagram B indicate the folds on your fabric.

With one long side of fabric towards you, trace section of the design from your prepared drawing diagonally on to lower right-hand quarter. To complete design, trace upper left-hand quarter to correspond.

Work embroidery following stitch and colour key and diagram A. All unnumbered parts on the stitch and colour diagram are

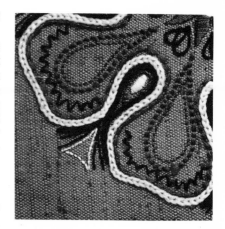

STITCHES

Stem stitch
Back stitch
Satin stitch
Couching
Chain stitch
Fly stitch
Buttonhole stitch

Bathroom set

worked in the same stitch and colour as the numbered parts most similar to them.

To make toilet seat cover. Cut one piece from turquoise fabric 24in. square. Trace large circular motif only centrally on to fabric, and work embroidery in a similar way as for bath mat.

STITCH AND COLOUR KEY
(**Note.** T indicates Tapisserie wool)

T1	Cyclamen Stem stitch
2	Cyclamen Stem stitch
T3	Black Stem stitch
4	Black Stem stitch
T5	Cyclamen Back stitch
6	Cyclamen Back stitch
7	White Back stitch
8	Black Back stitch
9	Cyclamen Satin stitch
10	White Satin stitch
T11	Cyclamen Couching
T12	White Couching
T13	White Chain stitch
14	White Chain stitch
T15	Black Fly stitch
16	Black Fly stitch
17	Cyclamen Buttonhole stitch

TO COMPLETE
Press embroidery on the wrong side.

Bath mat. Place embroidered piece, right side up, on to foam interlining, trim and oversew edges to keep in position. Make a row of tacking stitches 1in. from edge of turquoise fabric, as a guide line.

Cut one piece from towelling 23in. by 33in. for backing. Place embroidered fabric and interlining centrally on to towelling, turn surplus towelling over fabric to form a border on the right side, turn in $\frac{1}{2}$-in. hems, mitre corners, and slipstitch securely in position along tacking stitch guide line.

Toilet seat cover. Make a paper pattern of seat top, cutting straight across hinge section. Place pattern centrally on the wrong side of embroidered piece; trim away excess fabric, allowing $3\frac{1}{2}$in. extra on sides and front, and $\frac{3}{4}$in. on hinge edge. Turn back $\frac{1}{2}$in. hem on hinge edge, and stitch neatly. Turn in and machine the remaining edges to form a $\frac{1}{2}$-in. channel. Insert elastic through channel, draw up to fit and secure ends.

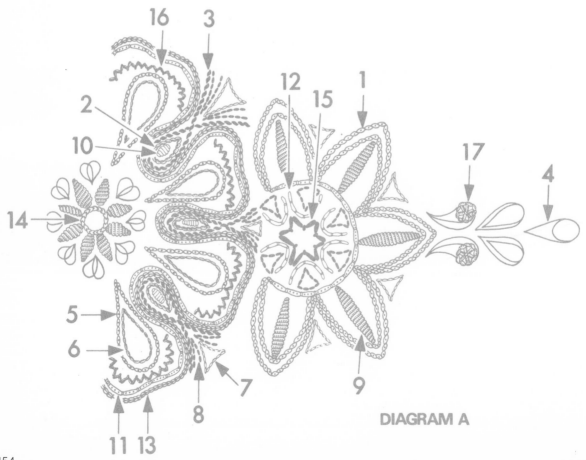

DIAGRAM A

Motif for child's dress

STITCHES
Stem stitch
Back stitch
Fern stitch
Detached chain stitch
Satin stitch
French knots
Buttonhole knots
Fly stitch
Straight stitch
Feather stitch

MATERIALS
Of Clark's Anchor Stranded Cotton—1 skein each of Nasturtium 0329/544, Cobalt Blue 0132/509, White 0402, and Parrot Green 0253/461. A plain-coloured dress to tone or contrast with embroidery thread shades. 1 Milward 'Gold Seal' crewel needle No. 6.

DIAGRAMS
Diagram A gives the complete motif in actual size.
Diagram B (page 158) gives a guide to the stitches and thread colours used throughout the design.

TO MAKE
Note. Use 3 strands throughout.
Trace motif from diagram A on to dress front 3in. from right-hand side seam and $4\frac{1}{4}$in. from lower edge.
Work embroidery following stitch and colour key and diagram B. All unnumbered parts on the stitch and colour diagram are worked in the same stitch and colour as the numbered parts most similar to them.

TO COMPLETE
Press embroidery on the wrong side.

DIAGRAM A

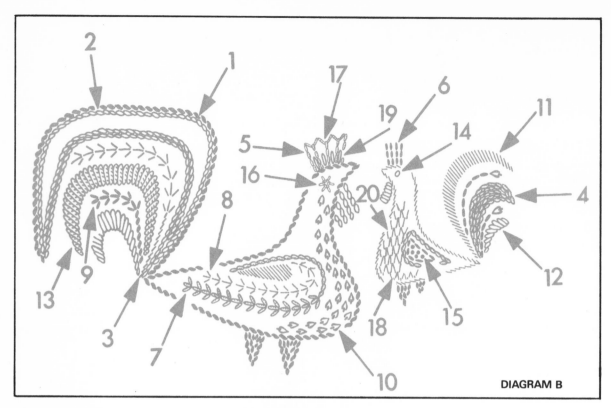

DIAGRAM B

STITCH AND COLOUR KEY

1 Cobalt Blue Stem stitch
2 White Stem stitch
3 Nasturtium Stem stitch
4 Parrot Green Stem stitch
5 Parrot Green Back stitch
6 Cobalt Blue Back stitch
7 Parrot Green Fern stitch
8 Nasturtium Fern stitch
9 Cobalt Blue Fern stitch
10 Cobalt Blue Detached chain stitch

11 Nasturtium Satin stitch
12 White Satin stitch
13 Parrot Green Satin stitch
14 White French knots
15 Cobalt Blue French knots
16 White Buttonhole stitch
17 Parrot Green Fly stitch
18 Nasturtium Fly stitch
19 White Straight stitch
20 Nasturtium Feather stitch

Motif for
an apron

MATERIALS
Of Clark's Anchor Stranded Cotton—2 skeins each of Magenta 063, Parrot Green 0254, and Almond Green 0263. A poplin apron in bright blue (or any colour wished). 1 Milward 'Gold Seal' crewel needle No. 7.

DIAGRAMS
Diagram A gives one large and one small motif in actual size.
Diagram B gives a guide to the stitches and thread colours used throughout the design. (Both diagrams on page 160.)

TO MAKE
Note. Use 3 strands throughout.
Fold the apron in half widthwise and crease lightly to mark the fold. With lower edge of apron facing you, trace the large and small motifs as given on diagram A, 2in. to the right of centre fold and $1\frac{1}{4}$in. from lower edge. Trace the large motif once more to the right of the small motif, and spacing it so it is a similar distance from the small motif as the first large motif.
Trace left-hand side of apron to correspond. Trace the small motif only centrally on to the waistband of apron. Trace 2 more small motifs to the right of the centre motif, and 2 more

STITCHES
Back stitch
Stem stitch
Straight stitch
Satin stitch
Double knot stitch
French knots

to the left of the centre motif, spacing motifs evenly 2in. apart. Work embroidery following stitch and colour key and diagram B. All unnumbered parts on the stitch and colour diagram are worked in the same stitch and colour as the numbered parts most similar to them.

TO COMPLETE

Press embroidery on the wrong side.

DIAGRAM A

STITCH AND COLOUR KEY
1 Magenta Back stitch
2 Almond Green Back stitch
3 Parrot Green Stem stitch
4 Parrot Green Straight stitch
5 Magenta Satin stitch
6 Almond Green Double knot stitch
7 Almond Green French knots

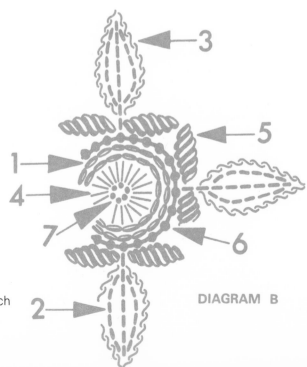

DIAGRAM B

Floral picture

MATERIALS

Of Clark's Anchor Stranded Cotton—1 skein each of Geranium 06, Azure (light) 0153, Azure (medium) 0155, Grass Green (light) 0241, Grass Green (medium) 0243, Buttercup 0295, Nasturtium 0329, Grey 0398, White 0402, Light Olive (tapestry shade) 0842, Medium Olive (tapestry shade) 0844, Dark Olive (tapestry shade) 0846, Medium Rose (tapestry shade) 0895 and Dark Rose (tapestry shade) 0896. $\frac{1}{4}$yd. fine embroidery linen in beige (or colour required), 36in. wide. A picture frame with mounting board or cardboard, 5in. by 7in. 1 Milward 'Gold Seal' crewel needle No. 6.

STITCHES

Stem stitch
Satin stitch
Long and short stitch
Straight stitch
Detached chain stitch
Buttonhole stitch
French knots

DIAGRAM A

DIAGRAMS
Diagram A gives complete design in actual size.
Diagram B gives a guide to the stitches and thread colours used throughout the design.

TO MAKE
Note. Use 3 strands throughout.
Cut one piece from fabric 9in. by 11in. Trace design from diagram A centrally on to fabric.
Work embroidery following stitch and colour key and diagram B. All unnumbered parts on the stitch and colour diagram are worked in the same stitch and colour as the numbered parts most similar to them.

TO COMPLETE

Press embroidery on the wrong side. Place embroidery centrally on mounting board, fold surplus fabric to the back and secure with pins into the edge of the board. Secure at the back by lacing side edges together with strong thread, and then lacing top and bottom edges together. Remove pins and place picture in frame.

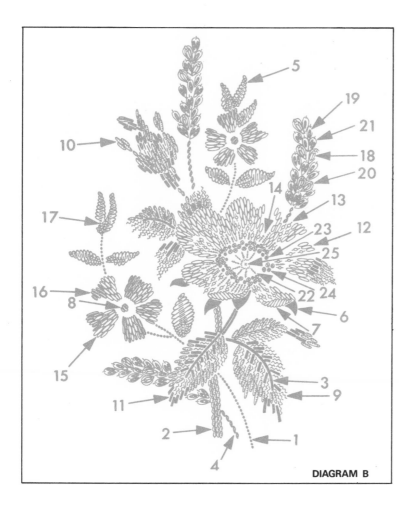

DIAGRAM B

STITCH AND COLOUR KEY

1 Medium Grass Green Stem stitch
2 Medium Olive Stem stitch
3 Dark Olive Stem stitch
4 Medium Olive Stem stitch
5 Light Grass Green Satin stitch
6 Dark Olive Satin stitch
7 White Satin stitch
8 Medium Azure Satin stitch
9 Light Olive Long and short stitch
10 Medium Olive Long and short stitch
11 Dark Olive Long and short stitch
12 White Long and short stitch
13 Geranium Long and short stitch
14 Grey Long and short stitch
15 Light Azure Long and short stitch
16 Medium Azure Long and short stitch
17 Light Grass Green Straight stitch
18 White Straight stitch
19 Dark Rose Straight stitch
20 White Detached chain stitch
21 Medium Rose Detached chain stitch
22 Grey Buttonhole stitch
23 Buttercup French knots
24 Nasturtium French knots
25 Grey French knots

Smocked dress

STITCHES
Stem stitch
Chevron stitch
Wave stitch
Satin stitch

MATERIALS
For a dress to fit a 4-5 year old child: of Clark's Anchor Stranded Cotton—1 skein each of Orange 0324/966, Oak Brown 0357/480 and Snuff Brown 0375/814. Pattern for a child's long-sleeved dress suitable for smocking. Fine wool or other fabric in mustard (or colour required)—amount quoted in the pattern. 1 reel Coats Satinised/Super Sheen No. 40 to match fabric. 1 Milward 'Gold Seal' crewel needle No. 6.

DIAGRAMS

Diagram A (page 166) shows a section of smocking design in actual size. The dotted lines at the left-hand edge indicate the rows of gathers and show the placing of smocking stitches in relation to these rows. The broken vertical lines indicate the folds formed when the gathering threads are drawn up.

Diagram B indicates the position of rows of running stitches.

Diagram C shows how to work stem stitch: this is worked from left to right, with the thread over 2 folds of fabric, but pick up only the top of one fold with the thread always kept below the needle.

Diagram D shows how to work chevron stitch: work from left to right, as in fig. 1. Begin with needle to the left of first pleat. Take stitch straight across first and 2nd pleats, with thread below needle. Bring needle out to left of 2nd pleat, above stitch just made. Keeping thread below needle, take next stitch across 3rd pleat but insert needle on gathering line above. Bring needle out to left of 3rd pleat. With thread above needle, stitch over 3rd and 4th pleats, bringing needle out to left of 4th pleat, below stitch. Now take thread back down to lower line and stitch across 5th pleat, bringing needle out to the left of it. Continue in this way. Fig. 2 shows a 2nd row of chevron stitch worked in reverse to form diamond pattern.

Diagram E shows how to work wave stitch: work from left to right, as shown in fig. 1. Begin with needle to the left of first pleat. Take stitch straight across first and 2nd pleats, with thread below needle. Bring needle out to left of 2nd pleat above stitch just made. Continue in this way until 6th pleat is reached. Have thread above needle for this stitch and bring needle out to left of 6th pleat, just below stitch. Work downward slope to correspond with upward. Fig. 2 shows the 2nd row of wave stitches worked in reverse to form diamond pattern.

TO MAKE

Note. Use 3 strands throughout.

Cut out dress, using paper pattern. Trace the design on to the wrong side of bodice front section, beginning $\frac{3}{4}$in. in from top and side edges. Use as much of the design as you need for the dress size you are making. Repeat design across width of fabric ending $\frac{3}{4}$in. from other side.

Now work running stitches across the dotted lines as in diagram B. Begin at right-hand side with a knot and back stitch to secure and gather by picking up a small portion of the fabric on each dot. Use a new thread for each row, and leave ends loose. Draw up threads, easing gently to form pleats as shown, but do not pull too tightly. Tie loose ends firmly in pairs close to the last pleat.

Work smocking stitches, following key to stitches and colours and diagram A.

Work section of design within brackets on diagram A on each sleeve, approximately $2\frac{1}{4}$in. from lower sleeve edge, substituting Oak Brown for Orange to work rows of stem stitch.

TO COMPLETE

Press smocking very lightly on the wrong side over a damp cloth. Remove all gathering threads and make up dress.

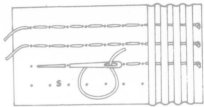

DIAGRAM B

DIAGRAM C

DIAGRAM D

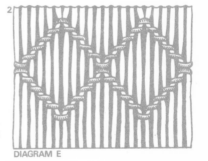

DIAGRAM E

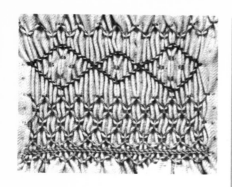

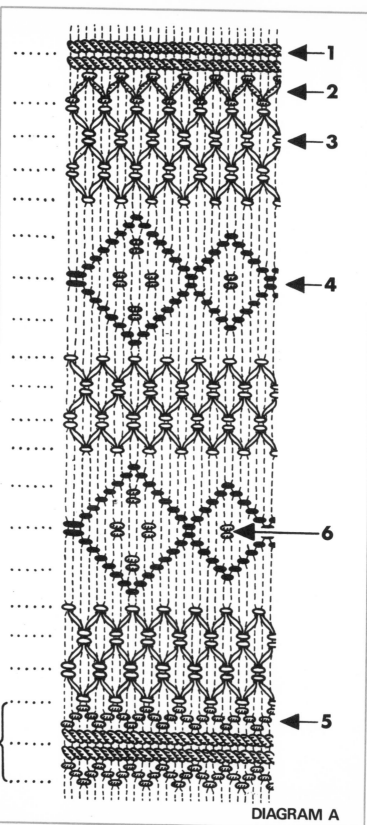

STITCH AND COLOUR KEY
1 Orange Stem stitch
2 Orange Chevron stitch
3 Snuff Brown Chevron stitch
4 Oak Brown Wave stitch
5 Orange Wave stitch
6 Orange Satin stitch

DIAGRAM A

MATERIALS

Of Clark's Anchor Stranded Cotton—6 skeins each of White 0402 and Black 0403, 2 skeins each of Amber Gold (medium) 0307 and Amber Gold (dark) 0309, and Orange 0325. ⅜yd. yellow mediumweight evenweave linen, 59in. wide, 21 threads to 1in. 1 Milward 'Gold Seal' tapestry needle No. 21.

DIAGRAM

Diagram A (page 168) gives half one short side of design, and three of the small motifs used on long sides. The background lines on the diagram represent the threads of the fabric.

TO MAKE

Note. Use 6 strands throughout.
Cut 3 pieces from fabric, each 13½in. by 17½in. Mark centres on each piece both ways with a line of basting stitches. The blank arrow on diagram A should coincide with the lengthwise basting stitches. Turn diagram sideways so it is the right way up. Work embroidery following key to colours, and taking straight vertical stitches across threads of fabric as indicated on diagram A. With one short side of fabric facing, commence at blank arrow 103 threads down from crossed basting stitches and work section given. Repeat in reverse from blank arrow to complete one short side. Continue small motifs on long sides to widthwise basting stitches. Turn fabric and repeat on other half to complete the design.

TO COMPLETE

Press the embroidery on the wrong side. Trim margins evenly. Turn back ½-in. hems, mitre corners and slipstitch.

Florentine table mats

(illustrated in colour on page 144)

STITCH

Florentine

DIAGRAM A

/ Medium Amber Gold

o Dark Amber Gold

● Orange

White

Black

MATERIALS

Of Clark's Anchor Stranded Cotton—3 skeins Laurel Green 771 and 1 skein Scarlet 469. ½yd. evenweave embroidery linen in yellow, 50in. wide, 21 threads to 1in. 1 Milward 'Gold Seal' tapestry needle No. 23. A cushion pad, approx. 17in. square.

Spanish blackwork cushion

DIAGRAM A

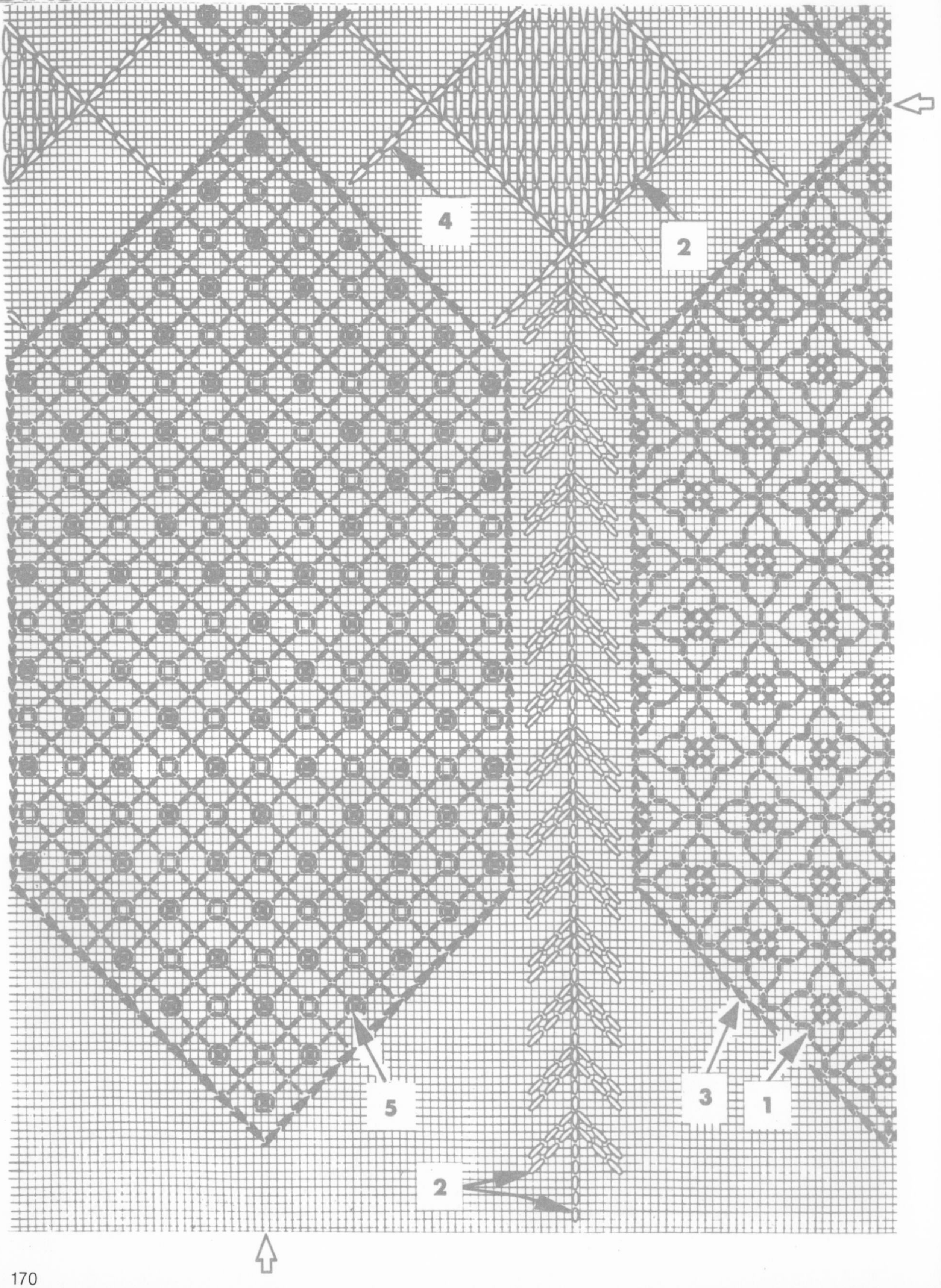

DIAGRAMS

Diagram A shows the arrangement of the stitches on the threads of the fabric. Each of the small background squares on the diagram represents one thread of the fabric. The section of design shown represents one central panel, and half of one right-hand panel, with a back stitch strip between.

TO MAKE

Note. Use 3 strands throughout.

Cut 2 pieces from fabric, each 18in. square. Mark one piece across the centre both ways with a line of basting stitches. The blank arrows on diagram A should coincide with the basting stitches worked on your fabric.

Work embroidery as indicated by stitch and colour key.

Work the section given first, then complete right-hand panel and another back stitch strip to correspond. Complete rest of embroidery as shown in photograph on page 169.

TO COMPLETE

Press embroidery on the wrong side. Place 2 fabric pieces together, right sides facing, and machine stitch round three sides, ½in. from edge. Press seam and turn right side out. Insert cushion pad, fold in turnings along remaining edge and slipstitch edges together.

STITCH AND COLOUR KEY

1 Laurel Green Back stitch
2 Scarlet Back stitch
3 Laurel Green Chain stitch
4 Scarlet Chain stitch
5 Laurel Green Cross stitch

STITCHES

Back stitch
Chain stitch
Cross stitch

Book list

The following list represents a good general selection of books on the art and technique of embroidery published since the 19th century. The recently published titles should be readily available through most booksellers. The older books however may not be so easy to obtain, but are well worth trying to track down. Alternatively, the books can usually be consulted at most good reference libraries.

Anchor Manual of Needlework
Batsford

American Needlework, G. B. Harbeson
Bonanza

Art of Embroidery,
Schuette and Müller-Christensen
Thames and Gudson

Complete Book of Needlework
Ward Lock

Craft of Embroidery, A. Liley
Mills and Boon

Crewel Embroidery, E. Wilson
Scribners

Design in Embroidery, K. Whyte
Batsford-Branford

Domestic Needlework, Seligman and Hughes
London 1926

East European Costumes, M. Tilke
Ernest Benn

Ecclesiastical Embroidery, B. Dean
Batsford

Embroidery (quarterly publication)
Embroiderers Guild

Embroidery—A Fresh Approach, A. Liley
Mills and Book

Embroidery Stitches, B. L. Snook
Batsford

English Needlework, A. F. Kendrick
A. & C. Black

History of English Embroidery, B. Morris
H.M.S.O.

Ideas for Machine Embroidery, E. Mason
Mills and Boon

Inspiration for Embroidery, C. Howard
Batsford

Learning to Embroider, B. L. Snook
Batsford

Machine Embroidery, J. Gray
Batsford

Mediterranean and Near Eastern Embroidery,
A. J. B. Wace
Halton

Needlework Through the Ages, M. Symonds
London 1928

Samplers, A Colby
Batsford

Encylcopedia of Needlework, Thérèse de Dillmont
D.M.C. Library, Mulhouse, France

Every Woman's Encylcopedia
London 1910

The History of Needlework Tools and Accessories, Sylvia Groves
The Hamlyn Publishing Group

Dictionary of Needlework,
S. F. A. Caulfeild and B. C. Saward
L. Upcott Gill, London 1903

Weldon's Practical Needlework
London c. 1900

Creative Embroidery, Christine Risley
Studio Vista

Heritage Embroidery, Else S. Williams
Van Nostrand Reinhold

A History of Western Embroidery,
Mary Eirwen Jones
Studio Vista

Acknowledgements

Acknowledgements are due to the following people and organisations who generously loaned work or photographs from their collection, for inclusion in this book:

Victoria and Albert Museum, London: Chinese picture, page 8; chasuble, page 10; cope, page 11; Italian cutwork sample, page 12; Italian whitework sample, page 13; Spanish blackwork sample, page 15; Elizabethan cover, page 19; drawn-thread sampler, page 21; patchwork cover, page 24; whitework sample, page 25; Norwegian sample, page 30; Swedish sample, page 33; Greek costume, page 38; Hungarian sample, page 41; Roumanian sample, page 42; Albanian cross stitch costume, page 82; cutwork sample, page 86; drawn-thread sampler, page 95; Danish shawls, page 100.
City of Manchester Art Galleries: broderie anglaise petticoat, page 27; croquet dress, page 31.
London Museum: Viking bone needle, page 6; selection of Roman materials, page 7; embroidered purse, page 12; Tudor caps, page 14; gloves and nightgown, page 16; stumpwork tray and Jacobean bed, page 22; christening robe, page 23; silk dress, page 25; apron and pincushion, page 26; waistcoat, page 40; beaded bag, page 70; silk shoes, page 78; gold dress, page 84.
Contemporary Hangings (exhibition organiser: Mrs. Vera Sherman): 'Cow Parsley', by Valerie Tulloch, page 28; 'Suspension', by Joy Clucas, page 29; 'The Spinney', by Vera Sherman, page 66; 'The Fountain', by Eirian Short, page 143; 'Gold Development' and 'Firmament', both by Joy Clucas, page 143.
Wm. Briggs and Co. Ltd.: Penelope designs illustrated on pages 71, 108 and 126. These designs are available as complete needlework kits from store needlework departments and needlework shops.
The Singer Company (UK) Ltd., Consumer Products Division: machine embroidery on page 102.
Mrs. D. Green, Orpington, Kent: goldwork design, on page 50; three kings, page 72; goldwork box, page 74.
Mrs. M. Craske, Hayes, Kent: tea cosies on pages 76 and 88; blackwork design, page 79; cushion, page 79.
Embroiderers Guild, London: design on page 93.
J. & P. Coats Ltd., all designs to make in the chapter beginning on page 104.

All other examples shown are from the collection of **Barbara Snook.**

Index

USA EQUIVALENTS

In general, needle sizes in the USA are the same as those used in the United Kingdom. Thread qualities however vary slightly: in the USA, as a rule, threads are divided into fine mercerised, ordinary mercerised and heavy duty. Fine mercerised should be used with fine and sheer fabrics; ordinary with all medium-weight fabrics; heavy duty for thick and weighty fabrics and most furnishing fabrics. There are good-quality multi-purpose threads available both in the UK and the USA which can be used with all fabric types and weights.

If Clark's Anchor Stranded Cotton is not readily available, then J & P Coats Deluxe Six Strand Floss can be substituted, and will give satisfactory results. The colour range is wide, and there should be an equivalent shade for each shade of Anchor Stranded Cotton. If Coats Anchor Tapisserie Wool is not readily available, then any good-quality tapestry wool can be satisfactorily substituted.